HOLIDAY
in
Hell

HOLIDAY
in
Hell

By Chico Holiday
With Bob Owen

Library of Congress
Catalog Card Number: 73-92387

Melodyland Productions
Anaheim, California

*To my wife Sally who prayed for me like
a hacking cough . . .*

CONTENTS

"I PREDICT . . ."
(NOTE: *Don't read the book till you read this!*)

The first time I met Chico Holiday, heard a bit of his story, and heard him sing, I realized that Chico is a professional in every respect. *But he is far, far more than that.*

The amazing thing about Chico is that he shares Jesus everywhere—including some of the top night spots in the entertainment world. As you read, and rub shoulders with Chico and Sally, the Holy Spirit Who possesses them will use their changed lives to change yours.

When you finish this book, prayerfully give it away. (In fact, get several and give them all away.) Because I predict that this true story will not only affect you, but everyone who reads it.

—Dr. Ralph Wilkerson, Pastor
Melodyland Christian Center

1

Jackpot

Labor Day weekend at Las Vegas, Sin City, U.S.A. *Look out! Everybody's gonna get rich!* I'm walking up on the stage at one of the big hotels ready to do my last show.

As I walk past the crap table I nearly stumble over a guy. He's stretched out on the floor. Then I see guards coming with oxygen and a stretcher. So I ask the pit boss, "Hey, Tony, what happened?"

Now Tony's all class. "Oh," he says, "he was dead before he hit the floor."

"Maybe we'd better hold the show. Or at least wait till they get the poor guy out of here. What do ya think?"

People are stepping over him like he was a bag of rags or something. One guy's straddling over him while he shoots dice — and begs God to "Give me an eight!"

I can't believe it.

Tony laughs. "Wait? What for? You're not gonna bother him. Go ahead. Do the show!"

So there we are — this guy lying there dead. And

me looking down at him. And Tony says, "Sing!" But I know Tony and I don't argue with him. I just kind of walk a little slower getting to the stage.

Backstage I tell the guys about it. Their eyes bugged out. "You're puttin' me on!" (Like all musicians, they're kind of spooky.)

"No I'm not. He's out there on the floor. Dead."

"We'd better hold off."

"No. They want us to do the show. Now!"

The guys just looked at me. They couldn't believe it. And, as a matter of fact, neither could I.

I said, "Look, we'll just take our time. Make like you're tuning up or something."

So we're just messing around, tuning, hoping they'll get that guy out of there before we start. And pretty soon here comes the stage manager. Clump, clump, clump. Running up the steps to the stage.

"Hey, come on you guys . . .!"

"Okay! Okay! We're ready."

"Well quit messin' around. What're you doin' anyway? You're five minutes late. C'mon — get it on!"

So I gave the signal and the boys hit it. As they do the curtain starts up. The music begins to build. And when the curtain hits right about at my shoulders I start singing. By the time I'm into the song, the curtain's all the way up.

This time, though, as it's going up all of us are leaning over, peeking under, seeing if the guy's still there.

The music's going, "Dum, de-de-dum . . . " The curtain gets to my shoulders and I sing, "What now, my love . . . de-de-de-dum . . ."

And we see him! They're carrying the guy out! They've got a sheet over him. His arms are hanging down, swinging back and forth. Like he's conducting! It made me sick to my stomach.

I thought, *Oh, Man! Do I really need this?*

Afterwards I got hold of Tony in the coffee shop. "You guys are cold . . . ! You've got no heart at all!"

He laughs. "That ain't nuthin'!"

So he tells about finding a little old lady back in the corner of one of the clubs by the slot machines. She's dead — her hand still gripped on the handle of the machine. Rigor mortis has already set in. Nobody'd noticed her. Or at least hadn't bothered to report it.

"She'd been there for hours," he said. "We had to take the machine apart and break her fingers to get her loose . . ."

He told me some more . . . and it made my blood run cold. Like the woman they finally located after her husband had been dead for three hours. Repeated pagings on the public address had failed to bring her to the office, or even pick up a house phone.

Finally one of the change girls said, "I think that's her over there. She's been there all day. I'm sure it's his wife."

So one of the managers approaches her. She's really engrossed in her game. She's got hold of a tandem machine (two machines hooked together — you feed a quarter into both sides, then pull the handle). The end result of one of those things: you can lose your bank roll twice as fast. Get out of town twice as early. Beat the traffic home. *And tell*

9

everybody what a great time you had in Vegas . . .

A monster like that never stops as long as you feed it. And she's been feeding it alright. Her white gloves are black from the coins. Her face is flushed and she's breathing hard. She's pumping that thing like her life depends on it.

"Uh, Mrs. Johnson . . . "the manager begins.

"Yeah. Whadaya want?" She doesn't turn her head. She just keeps feeding that monster. *Feed . . . jerk. Feed . . . jerk. Clang, clung, clang.*

"Didn't you hear us paging you?"

"Yeah, I heard."

"Well, why didn't you answer? We just asked you to pick up one of the white phones . . . "

Angrily. "I was busy. I'm still busy! What's on your mind?"

"Well, it's about your husband . . . "

"What about my husband?"

No pause. *Feed . . . jerk. Clang, clung, clang. Feed . . . jerk. Clang, clung . . .*

"We'll, what is it? Tell me!" *Feed . . . jerk. Feed . . . jerk.*

"We'd like to talk to you in back. It's pretty serious . . ."

"Well, what happened? Just shut up and tell me. I'm not leavin' this machine. I've been feedin' it all day. And it's about to hit."

Feed . . . jerk. Clang . . .

The manager takes a deep breath. "Uh, Mrs. Johnson, your husband's had a heart attack."

Feed . . . jerk. Feed . . .

"Mrs. Johnson, I said . . ."

"I heard you! How is he?" No sign of emotion.

No let up.

"Frankly, Mam, he's dead . . ."

No flicker of an eyelash. No answer. *Feed . . . jerk.*

"Uh, Mrs. Johnson, like I said, he's . . ."

"I heard you!" *Feed . . . jerk.* "I told the big slob he couldn't take it." *Feed . . . jerk . . .*

The manager's seen and heard about everything. But this really gets to him. He just stands there. He can't believe it.

"I told the dummy to stay home," she finally says. "He knew he had a bad heart . . . "

At that precise moment the bells ring and quarters start pouring out. She grabs them and starts scooping them into her bag. "I knew it . . . I told ya. Jackpot. *Jackpot!*"

The manager left her there, frantically filling her pockets and purse with the glittering coins. *In the lounge her dead husband was already cold.* But she didn't care about that — her machine was hot — she'd finally hit the jackpot.

They called an ambulance and took him away. There was nothing else they could do.

I kept thinking about that dead guy they carried out while I sang that night. His arms swinging. And I wondered who he was. I wondered if he had a wife. And if she was at home. Or if she was yanking the handle of one of those one-armed bandits.

Some would say, "Well, that's show business."

But after a while it gets to you. You're really into it. You give every performance all you've got. Then the act's over. And you realize nobody really knows you . . .

11

That you're only as good as your last perform-ance, and the public's got an awful short memory.

But show business is in your blood.

I think I got inoculated with the show business disease that summer I got the job at Oakton Manor, a resort just outside Waukesha, Wisconsin that catered to people mostly from the Chicago area.

2

Show Business

I knew I was in it now. And my mind was whirling as I stared at the fat little guy — smoking one of those short stinky cigars. He was shaking his stubby finger under my nose.

"Hey! Hey, Mister Life Guard. Ya deef or sumpin'? I ax ya a question!"

I shook my head, sorta dazed like.

"Uh, yeah. Uh, whacha say?"

"I ax if ya give swimmin' lessons."

At that moment I would gladly have given up all thoughts of a career in show business — even before I got started.

I took a deep breath. "I'm sorry. But I don't give swimming lessons."

His fat little daughter Debra was standing there looking sassy. I'd seen her around. And the last thing I wanted to do was to try and teach her how to survive in the water. Or any place else for that matter.

"Ya what?" he shouts, his neck veins turning purple.

"Look, Mister Life Guard, I'm payin' $42.50 a

13

day at this place. And for that my daughter should learn to swim already now. I ax ya, is that expectin' too much?"

"Like I said, Sir, I don't give lessons."

He grabs Debra. and the two of them start wobbling away. Over his shoulder he fires this parting shot, "Okay, Mister Life Guard, I'll talk to the manager . . ."

In that split second, I saw Debra and me both drowning. I also saw my job going down the drain. I choked out, "Wait a minute!"

The guy turned. He'd chomped that cigar to shreds. He waits.

"Uh, I mean . . . can you bring her back after lunch?"

He looks at me with a kind of a sneer. "Okay. That's more like it. Yeah, sure. I'll bring the kid back after lunch. C'mon, Debra, let's go eat."

So while they go add another layer of fat, I rush into town and pick up a Red Cross manual on swimming.

When Debra comes back I'm ready for her. I get her into the shallow end of the pool, and I recite to her from the book. And, lo and behold, the dummy learns how to swim.

Her father was flabbergasted. She'd been going to camp for three summers, and never learned to swim. And here in just a couple of days she's swimming like a trout. Now this grateful father tells the manager what a good boy I was.

If you think he was surprised . . . nobody knew how surprised I was.

It was funny the way I got that job at Oakton

Manor. I suppose deep down I'd always wanted to get into show business. In fact, one of my dreams as a youngster was to be a trapeze artist in the circus. So (unbeknown to anybody) I started "practicing" out in a building my dad used for a training hall where he used to work the dogs in bad weather. We had a kennel where we boarded and trained all kinds of dogs — my dad was the best trainer I ever saw.

Well, one day my mother came out to get me for something. She didn't know anything about my trapeze dreams. When she walked in I was hanging by my heels on the bar — about twenty feet off the ground. I guess she thought I was up in the loft or something, because when she opened the door she looked in and yelled, *"Are you up there?"*

And I yelled back, "Yeah. Up here!"

She looked up and saw me hanging by my heels on that bar. And — boom! Out like a light. Fainted.

As far as singing goes — well I tried out for the high school chorus. And they said, "Don't call us. We'll call you."

I joined the high school band and played the French horn — mostly by ear again — and got straight B's. But I never played the guitar until my last year of high school. I knew this German family, friends of mine, especially Jerry and Bob Hoffsteder. These guys were really talented. Really good.

They put together a show that was really in demand for picnics and dances and stuff. One day they said, "Hey, Chico. Come and play the guitar with us. A jam session . . ."

I guess that's where it all really started. I got so I liked playing around on the guitar. I wasn't much good, but I liked it, and we all had a lot of fun.

One day Jerry and Bob said, "Hey, Chico, we've got this assembly at high school . . ."

I saw what was coming and said, "Oh, no. You're not going to get me before that crowd."

You see, the only time I'd play and sing was with those guys, or with my cousins, Frankie and Jim Rutter. And then just at home or just fooling around. We'd get together and do Western and Country music. We'd put on a show for our family. But it was just kid stuff.

But they persisted that day. "C'mon. We'll do, 'Your Cheatin' Heart.' All you gotta know is these three chords . . . C, G and F. That's all. You can do it."

"Naw, I don't think so."

"Sure. Here grab the guitar. Just do these chords . . ."

That instant I grabbed the guitar that day and picked out those chords . . . well, that was the fatal moment. That was my undoing. Cause from that point on, I was hooked. A strung-out guitar junkie.

Anyway, we did the assembly. We wore blue pants, white shirts and red suspenders. The teacher about flipped. But the kids loved it. And I loved it too . . .

About that time a lot of things began to happen. There was this talent show the Kiwanis Club gave. My sister went to audition for it and I went with her. I saw some of the people, listened to them sing, and knew I could sing as good as they. So I went home and said to my mother, "I'm going to audition."

It surprised them all. But I auditioned and made

it. Man, that was great. Later I started singing with two young girls called "The Big Sisters." We even recorded a song they wrote. It was about the Boston Braves moving to Milwaukee. We called it the "Braveland Boogie." We sang around Milwaukee and got known a little bit.

Then one day I got a phone call from an agent. He said, "We've got an opening with the 'Grand Ol' Oprey Road Show' at the State Fair. We need a couple more people to beef up the show a little. You interested . . .?"

And so, being very super cool, I answered, "Y . . . e (gulp), ye . . . a . . . h."

They paid me $125 a week. But I'd have done it for nothing. I mean, who cares about money. Boy, it's experience. So they told me it wasn't quite what I thought it would be, you know, actually working with the stars. They had a big tent and all the Grand Ol' Oprey stars from Nashville were inside . . .

But that's where the 'association' began and ended. You see, I was on the outside — doing the ballyhoo. Our job was to get the folks inside to see and hear 'the real action.'

It was really great. This little bitty guy with a straw hat and sleeves rolled up (just like you see in the movies) would get up and begin to gather the crowd. He was really good. He'd begin yelling, "Okay, folks. Gather around everybody now. Hurry, hurry, hurry . . ."

And when the crowd began gathering, he'd give them this pitch: "Alright, folks. We're gonna put on just a little taste of what you're gonna see on the inside . . ."

So I'd go up there and start banging out a song called, "I Wanna, Wanna, Wanna, Some of Your Love . . ." And I'd get just about that far when the barker'd break in again.

"Here he is, Folks. A young star from Nashville, Tennessee. Just a taste of what you're gonna see and hear on the inside . . ."

I'd come in then with the song. And he'd come on strong again . . .

"Hold it right there. That's enough. We don't want to give them too much. Now, take down that 50c sign. And put up the 25c sign . . ."

And he'd begin crowding the people into the tent. We'd work this way from maybe ten in the morning till ten at night. And I thought, *Oh Boy, this is great!* But looking back now I say, "What a drag!"

When that was over I hit kind of a slump. I auditioned here and there, and sang a lot, but I was getting nowhere fast.

I was working in a steel mill. Pouring metal. It was tough work, but I was making good money. Thing was, though, it was dark when I went to work. And dark when I got home. It was tough singing when you're so tired. But I didn't mind. I was young.

I left that job after just a short time. Partly because I was too tired to sing much. But mainly because I saw one of the melting pots explode. It looked like Vesuvius going off. At that time I had graduated from pouring metal to running the five-ton overhead crane. But it scared me, that explosion. I didn't like all the dust and smoke and turmoil anyway.

I began working for the Music Center in Waukesha. And I guess that's where things really began for me. Not the music store, but what happened because of it. One day I was delivering a piano, and I drove past this resort called Oakton Manor. I remembered my father training a dog that belonged to the owner of that resort. It all came back to me then. Dad told me how they had floor shows there. And that they booked big acts from Chicago.

I thought, *Wow! That'd be something if I could get in there!* That was about the time when Dean Martin and Jerry Lewis had just made it. They'd been discovered working in the same type resorts in the Catskill Mountains. I knew that they and some other stars had made it going this route. Eddy Fisher, Buddy Hackett, and some others.

So after I delivered the piano I stopped there and asked them for a job. I told the manager about my show business aspirations. I said, "I know I'm not qualified to be in one of your shows. But if I could only get a job — doing anything — it would give me a chance to meet some of the performers . . . and, besides, I don't need much money . . ."

The manager's name was Sam Sugarman. He digested what I said and then said, "That sounds great."

My heart swelled till it almost broke in two, I was so happy.

"We've got Ranch Night Mondays," he went on in his clipped English accent. He had one of those little moustaches right out of a Flynn movie. (We used to call him the "Jewish Bengal Lancer" behind his back.) "You could play your guitar when there's nobody else."

He looked me over carefully. "Yeah, sounds okay. You could watch the shows at night."

"You'll hire me then?"

"Well, we've only got two jobs open. We need a busboy. And a life guard."

Like a flash I thought, *There's more class being a life guard.* But I never thought that some lives could literally depend on me. I said, "I'll take the life guard job."

He said, "Okay. We have midnight swims. And if you want to take your guitar down there and play and sing for the guests, that's fine. Why don't you go down and check out the pool . . ."

So I did. The guy down there showed me where the towels were. How to regulate the temperature of the water, and how to keep the pool clean. I was back upstairs in a couple of minutes.

"Mr. Surgarman . . . I . . . I'll take the job. I'll be your life guard."

He told me about the hours and the pay and that stuff, and told me when to report for work. I was about to leave, to go and quit my job at the Music Center, when he says, "One more thing . . . do you have a swimming suit?"

I didn't but I knew I could get one. So I lied, "Yeah, I've got one."

Driving back to Milwaukee it suddenly hit me what I'd done. I must have had more nerve than a toothache. It didn't bother me so much about the swimming suit. It was more than that. You see, the reason I didn't have a swimming suit was because *I didn't know how to swim!*

3

Don't Blow My Cover!

One of the first things I did was to get myself a long pole and make a hook on the end of it. I figured if anybody went down I could at least gaff them over to the edge. Then I could reach down and pull them out.

One day Mr. Sugarman was walking through the pool area, and he sees this big hook. In his "Errol-Flynn-British-accent" he says, "I say . . . what's that big hook?"

I had an answer ready for him. "Oh, ah . . . people come into the pool after they've been drinking at night. And sometimes throw lounge chairs in the water and stuff like that. So, instead of having to go and change clothes and fish 'em out . . . I just hook 'em out."

He nods in his precise way. "Oh, I say, that's very clever. That's what we like to see."

Looking back, I can see that Oakton Manor really was the beginning of things. Lots of times when I was "guarding" the pool, I'd be singing and playing. On talent nights I got in a lot of licks. And even after the shows on Saturday nights I'd be singing. We'd have jam sessions and stuff. And I was getting pretty popular.

I learned a lot at Oakton Manor. The people were good to me and I loved working with them. Of course, I was always ready, willing and able for that "big break" that show people are eternally awaiting.

Mine came in a way I could never have imagined.

After a while, Sam Sugarman promoted me to the position of Social Director. That was a big step. Of course, I was still the life guard, too. But now it was my responsibility to keep people happy *and* alive.

Among other things this meant that I was also the full-time singer at the Manor. Before this time they used to book in a three-act show: a comic, a dance team and a singer. Now they needed only the comic and the dancer. I took care of the singing.

Suddenly it occurred to me that *I had arrived*. I was the star at Oakton Manor. I was a full-time, full-fledged entertainer. At that time I didn't know the Lord, so I failed to give Him any thanks for it all. But I knew I had accomplished in a very short time what many entertainers were still trying to accomplish.

For instance, I learned that the *Chicago Tribune* was putting on an annual affair they called the "Harvest Moon Festival." It was sort of a contest for professionals. And the winner — *the winner* — would receive as his prize a two week booking at Oakton Manor.

And that's where Chico — me — a relatively "unknown"—was booked *full time*. When that fact sunk into my thick skull I was a pretty happy kid.

Man! I was swinging pretty high around there.

But then one day I came down to earth *hard*.

Though I was life guard, I still hadn't learned how to swim. During high school, Coach Candle had despaired over me. I could see him shaking his head over my efforts to stay afloat. I took only one semester of swimming during high school, but I flunked it. Well, really the coach let me slip by because he felt sorry for me, but he should have failed me completely.

Anyway I was really doing great at the Manor until the scouts came. Word came down from the office, "Open up the pool tonight for the bunch of scouts from Waukesha High School."

I didn't sweat it. I said, "Okay," and went down.

And who did I meet down there with the scouts. You guessed it. Coach Candle was the scout-master.

He looked surprised. "What are you doing here?"

I grinned. "I work here."

"You work here?"

"Yeah, I work here."

Then came the inevitable. "Uh, what do you do?"

I wasn't grinning now. "You'll never believe it . . ."

He turned pale. "You're not . . . you're not . . . the life guard?"

"I told you you wouldn't believe it."

"Chico, you're crazy! You're really crazy. You can't even swim . . .!"

"That's right . . . but, Coach . . . uh, please don't blow my cover . . ."

"Why not? You're liable to drown somebody!" He was really upset.

"Yeah, but I'm not going to be here very long.

23

I'm going to be quitting this job in a little while . . ."

He shook his head. He looked dazed. I guess it was quite a shock to the poor guy. "Well, okay," he says. "But this is terrible! Really terrible . . ." And he walks away shaking his head and muttering under his breath.

I noticed that he kept close tabs on the swimmers that night.

But another jolt was coming.

At that time there was a big radio show in Chicago called "Marty's Morgue." Run by Marty Faye, it was sort of like the "Tonight" show that's on TV now. Though it was a local show, it was very well known.

Marty Faye was famous for his sharp tongue. He could just cut a guy to ribbons. He had a record show, combined with interviews. He'd get performers to bring their records and he'd play them . . .

Sometimes in the middle of a record, you'd hear, "Scratch . . . smack!" when he'd jerk it off the turntable and smash it across the console.

"That's the worst record I've ever heard!"

Or, "Do you really think you're any good?"

His opinion could bury people. But if he liked you, you were made. I knew all this, though I had never seen the man.

One Saturday night just before the show someone came up and said, "Marty Faye's out front."

And I thought, *Oh, Man . . .!*

I knew he was liable to stand up right in the middle of my first number and shout, "Get that bum off! He stinks . . . he stinks like yesterday's fish!"

I was scared stiff all through the show. But everything went along okay. Later I was relaxing when somebody said, "Marty Faye wants to talk to you."

I didn't know the Lord at this time, like I said earlier, and I was scared, not knowing what to expect. So I went over to his table.

He looked me over. "Hey, Kid . . . you're pretty good . . ."

To me that was like having the Pope come up and kiss me on the forehead, or the president inviting me to lunch.

So I said, very reserved and cool like, "Th . . . a . . . a . . . nk yo . . . u . . . (gulp, gulp) ve . . . r . . . y much."

He didn't seem to notice my extreme cool. But says, "I tell you what. I got some friends at Mercury. And I might be able to do you some good. Put a few songs on a dub (demonstration record) and send it to me. And I'll send it to them. And we'll see what happens."

I knew what this could mean. Quite literally, if Marty Faye would send someone a record and say, "I think this kid is really great . . ." you're in!

Somehow I kept my semblance of cool, thanked him and got back to my room. I don't remember what I did then, but I kind of came apart at the seams. I knew that this might be the biggest break of my short career.

I did what he said. I made a dub, and had about four extra copies made. I sent the first one to him. I also made a list of all the major recording companies (by searching through all the trade papers — *Cash Box, Billboard, Variety, Record World,* and others) and sent a dub to them. Along with it I sent a resume and a picture of myself, addressed to the A and R men (Artist and Repertoire) or producers.

And you know what response I got? Right. "Don't call us. We'll call you." I got batches of stock rejections slips that said something like: "Thank you for sending us your material. However, due to . . . (every reason in the world) we are returning it. Please don't think because of this that your voice has no merit . . ."

That didn't discourage me though (like fun it didn't), so I'd immediately stick the package together again, get a new name from my list and mail it to someone else.

So there I was, plugging along at Oakton Manor. Enjoying myself. Happy but not satisfied. Then one day I got a phone call from New York City. "Hello, Chico," the voice said.

"Yeah," I said, "I'm Chico."

"My name is Larry Auerback. I represent the William Morris Agency . . ."

When he said that, I almost fainted. The William Morris Agency is probably one of the largest entertainment agencies in the world.

Somehow I kept my faculties, and in my usual very cool way I said, "'Y . . . e . . . (gulp, gulp) e . . . s."

"Chico, RCA Victor has asked me to invite you to New York to do some recording."

"You mean to audition?"

"No. To record. They've heard some things that you sent out. And they want to put you under contract . . ."

He paused, but I couldn't say a single word.

". . . how soon can you be here?"

4

You're Fired!

Things began happening fast after that. I mean really fast! I went to New York and recorded "Young Ideas." And it went about three quarters of a million. Which is pretty good for the first one. In fact, it isn't bad for any record.

After signing the contract with RCA one of the wheels came in and said, "Chico, how do you spell your last name?"

So I said, "It's V-e-r-g-o-l-i-n-o. Vergolino. But I call myself Verlin for short."

He said, "Forget it, Chico. We can't use that. No way! We've got to have something with real class. With charisma . . ."

So he got a bunch of the men together — the real brains of the outfit — and they kicked my name around. They had the Madison Avenue boys, the publicity guys for RCA, Hugo and Luigi — the two guys that would be producing all my sessions. And they began tossing names around.

"How about Johnny Dove?"

"Or Johnny October . . .?"

"Forget the Johnny bit," one guy said. "Chico's alright. But we've got to have something Anglo Saxon to balance it off."

Somebody said, "Chico Sunday . . . "

"Why don't we call it one of the holidays?" I said. "You know, like Chico Arbor Day? or Chico Yom Kippur . . . or something like that?" I was getting tired of not having a name.

"Hey, that's it?"

"Chico Arbor Day?" I asked.

"No. Chico Holiday. It fits. You know, entertainment — holiday. Holiday. Chico Holiday!"

I guess everybody was getting tired about that time. Anyway we kind of left it there hanging and went home. As I went out the door, though, one of the PR guys slapped me on the shoulder and said, "Good night, Chico. Chico Holiday!" Then he laughed. I wasn't too sure about it, but I didn't say anything.

But during the night I couldn't sleep very well. So the first thing in the morning I called up the manager and said, "You know, I don't think I like my name."

"What do you mean?" he said.

"Well, that Holiday part. Chico *Holiday*. I'm not so sure that I like the sound of it."

He laughed. "It's too late."

"Too late?"

"Yeah. Too late. We've got the publicity all printed and in the mail. We've got the record labels printed and slapped on."

"Man! You guys don't waste any time," I said.

"That's right. Sorry, Chico. Like it or not . . .

your name's Holiday now. Chico Holiday . . ."

I just said, "Thanks," and hung up. There wasn't much else I could do.. So, from then till now I've been Chico Holiday. But you know what? I've come to like it. Sometimes I have a rough time spelling Vergolino.

While I was with RCA I did the Dick Clark Show a number of times. Got a lot of exposure that way. After I'd been on the show about four or five times, Dick said, "Chico, let's talk about something different."

"Okay by me."

"What I mean," he went on, "is there anything you ever did that was really . . . you know . . . funny or different . . .?"

My manager spoke up, "Tell him about the life guard bit."

"Yeah . . . yeah! Good idea," I said. "You see, when I first went to the . . ."

That's as far as I got. Dick said, "Don't tell me till you get on the show. Because I want my reaction to be like everybody else's . . ."

So when we got before the cameras, I told him about my job at Oakton Manor as a "non-swimming-life-guard." Everybody got a good laugh out of it. But the punch line came about an hour later when a telegram came addressed to me, care of The Dick Clark Show. It read:

"Dear Chico, you're fired. Regards, Sam."

That was really funny, apparently they'd all known I was going to be on the show that day, and they had watched it. I was on leave of absence from the Manor at that time, but I think we all realized that I probably wouldn't be back there again to work. They were really beautiful people.

About that time I met Sally. Another terrific milestone in my life. I had a booking at the Metropole Supper Club in Windsor, Canada, right across the river from Detroit, Michigan. I was with my manager Simmy Bow one afternoon. We were on our way to do the rehearsal. All at once Simmy stops and waves at two girls. Up till that time I hadn't had much time for girls, and I really didn't know very many of them.

"Hey, I know those girls," he said.

"What's the difference?" I said.

"I wancha to meet them . . . one's a singer. And that one on the right . . . she's the dancer."

It turns out that Sally was the dancer.

We come up to them. Simmy says, "Hi, Sally. This is Chico."

"Hi, Chico."

"Hi, Sally . . ."

I don't know if it was a bolt of lightning or something. But something hit me.

"Uh . . ." Simmy says, "say, why don't you come to the rehearsal with us?"

Sally said, "No thanks. Not today."

But Gloria, Sally's friend, said, "Go on, Sally. You know you've got nothing to do this afternoon . . ."

Well, Sally was kind of on the spot. So she said, "Maybe you can drop me off on the way. I've got some things to do down town." We started talking and laughing, and before we knew it, we were in front of the club.

Sally was nice. I liked her. And I guess you might say something clicked. Anyway we were together almost constantly for the next two weeks. After that I had to go to Miami for a week, but she had an engagement in Europe . . .

We must have had it bad, because we kept Mr. Bell in change. One day I was in the middle of a recording session. The light went on and Luigi said, "Phone, Chico. For you. Long distance."

You're right. It was Sally. "Hi," she said.

"Where are you?" I asked.

"Laborador. Goosebay, Laborador . . ."

Another time the call came from a phone booth just outside Notre Dame Cathedral in Paris. I suppose it wasn't so different courting your girl by telephone. But from around-the-world-trans-Atlantic telephone? By the time she got back we had to get married. Neither one of us could handle phone bills like we had.

We finally got things worked out (by phone). I was working at that time in the Che Paris in Providence, Rhode Island. She was to meet me there, then we'd drive home and get married. And so we did . . . and lived happily (though often hectically) ever after. I learned that living with Sally you never know what's going to happen. More about that later.

By this time through mismanagement and bad advice I found myself in debt to the tune of $13,000 or more, and owing back commissions to agents all across the country. They wouldn't book me until they were paid and I couldn't pay them until I had some bookings. Things were going down, down, down . . . and my new Bonneville I'd just bought disappeared. Finally, I got booked into the *Che Parie* in Providence, Rhode Island, through some of our old connections. But now I needed transportation so I wound up with this old '52 Plymouth. It, too was something else. It ran pretty good (part of the time), even though the upholstery and paint were shot. And the tires were so thin you could see through them. (The only thing that worked on the car was the mechanic!)

Just as I got to the Club one of those tires went flat. So I just left it there at the curb and walked in.

I met the owners, Billy and Angelo. I said, "Hey, you know, my tire went flat. Just when I drove up."

"Too bad, Kid. Tough luck."

"Yeah, I know. The spare's no good. Where can I buy one?"

He looked at me funny like. "Buy one?" he asked. *"Buy a tire?"*

"Yeah, Angelo, like I told you, it's flat. And it's not worth fixin' . . . I need a new one."

He kind of shakes his head. Then he yells, "Hey, Junior . . .!"

And this big dude come lumbering out of the wings. He looks like a Neopolitan King Kong. Junior said, "Uh. Yuh, whadja want, Angelo?"

"This here's Chico."

The big guy crunches my hand. "Hi, Chico."

Angelo said, "The Kid here needs a tire. Get it for him."

Junior said, "What kind? What size?"

"My car's at the curb. Just something that'll fit it." He disappears and I forget him.

I was to go on that night so I was rehearsing with

the house band. And about an hour later the door opens up and here comes Junior. He's got these two tires under his arms. He comes right up on the stage and drops them. Thump . . . thump, thump, thump, thump . . ."

"This one here's a white-wall tubeless," he said. "And this other one's got a tube. But it's a good tire. It's got lottsa miles on it."

I knew enough not to ask where he got them. I learned later that he'd driven around Providence till he found a car the same make and model as mine. So he just took out his jack and pulled a wheel off. While he was double-parked there, taking off the second wheel, a cop came up.

He said, "What are you doing?"

Junior looks up, "A friend of mine's got a flat tire. I'm just fixing it for him."

So the cop directs traffic around him while he rips off with the second wheel.

And here they were, on the stage in front of me. I said, "I'll be glad to pay you for them . . ."

"Naw. Give me a glossy 8 by 10 and I'll be happy."

That was quite a club. I'll never forget it.

That New Year's night is one for the books. I opened up with a real hip arrangement of "Will You Still Be Mine?" The band was really into it, and they announce me offstage . . .

"Ladies and gentle . . . men. The Che Parie . . . is proud . . . to present R . . . C . . . A's . . . recording artist . . . Chico . . . Holiday . . .!"

And I make my entrance.

I was wearing my blue mohair tux, my monogrammed ruffled shirt with ruffled sleeves. And French cuffs. Patent leather shoes . . . a real swinger . . . I opens my mouth for the first number . . .

All of a sudden a chair goes flying across the room, clear from one side to the other. It hits a guy in the back of the head. He jumps up and responds with language that's hardly conducive to my opening number.

In seconds the place is in complete pandemonium.

I just stood there a minute, not knowing what to do. Finally I turn to the band leader and say, "Play my bow music."

He did, and I just walked off the stage. That was my first performance for the night. All of it.

That was rather typical of things that happened at that club. One Saturday night, for instance, I'm right into the show, and the owner comes up and gives me the cut sign. I finished the last song and cut. When I walked backstage I said, "What's going on?"

He said, "Chico, we're going to a wedding."

It was Saturday night, the busiest night of the week. The place was jammed. I thought the guy was nuts. I said, "Are you crazy? A wedding? We can't leave now!"

"Hey!" he said, "it's my place. If I say we go to a wedding, then we go . . ."

As we went out he says, "Don't worry, Kid. You'll finish your show at the wedding"

That wedding was something else.

5

Mafia

They held the wedding at another club. I think it was the owner's son or daughter who was getting married. The place was wide open. Everything was free.

They opened up the kitchen. They opened up the cigarette machine. They opened up the bar and put all the imported liquor where everybody could help themselves. Whatever anybody wanted was there. Free.

And over in one corner was a table stacked high with fur coats. Every kind of fur coat you could think of was there. It represented lots of money. *Lots of money!*

Then it hit me. It's a mob party. A sort of family thing. The Mafios were walking around in their starched fronts and collars looking impressive and uncomfortable. All of these guys are smoking those little Italian cigars the kind they soak in wine. (Like my grandfather smoked.)

Man! you inhale one of those things and it'll blow the top of your head off.

Something funny though. They had a champagne

fountain. It was gold plated. There were several tiers, and the champagne (the very best) was spraying out the top, all bubbly, and running down the sides of the tiers into the pool at the bottom. The air was so heavy and heady that you didn't have to drink the stuff. You got high just being in the room.

But this was the payoff: no glasses. You'd drink that expensive champagne out of ordinary Lily paper cups. They just didn't want to put out the imported champagne glasses. Didn't make sense to me. But that's how it was.

I tell you, I was used to working in the midst of confusion at the clubs. But this was something else. And, I did finish my show at the wedding.

They really liked me there at that club, and I liked them. And when Sally came and we told them we were getting married, the owners said, "Hey Chico. You and Sally come into the office. Okay?"

So we did. It was just a back room. They had cases of booze stacked around. They didn't trust anybody, only themselves. And they kept that "office" locked tight all the time. Over in the corner there was a little desk squeezed in. Hanging next to it was a beautiful $500 cashmere coat. It wasn't hanging on a hanger, but on a nail. And the nail's about to poke a hole through the back of it!

Angelo waves us to a couple of dusty chairs. "Sit down. Sit down."

He reached into the pocket of the cashmere coat and pulled out a long manila envelope. He ripped off the end and spilled the contents on the desk in front of him—a huge pile of diamond rings! I know they're hot. You could have fried eggs on them. I was surprised they didn't burn a hole through the desk.

He spread them out. The light reflected from those massive diamonds was blinding. They still had their tags on. There must have been at least a million dollars there!

Angelo stubbed out his cigar. "Here, Kid. Take a coupla dees. Use em fer yer weddin' ring . . ."

I gulped and looked at Sally. Her eyes were about as big as mine . . .

I didn't move. I couldn't.

"C'mon, Kid. Grab a couple."

I said, "Man! How can I do that? How can I ask a priest to bless something like that?"

He thought about that. 'Yeah, I guess you're right."

He picked up one of the largest stones, held the ring in his hand for a moment, admiring it. Then he pried the diamond out of the setting with his teeth. "Here," he said, handing it to me, "take the rock then . . ."

I shook my head. 'Thanks, Angelo, but I can't do that." I know he was just trying to be nice, but it was kind of strange.

He looked at us. He shrugged. "Well, I think you're nuts. But that's alright. Good luck to youse anyway . . ."

As I recall, that club was my first real taste of Mafia. But before long both Sally and me were into the middle of it. For some reason—I know now it was only God's protection—we never got hooked.

One of the top men got hold of me one day and made me an offer.

He said, "Chico, Baby. I like you. You're good. Ya know?"

I shrugged. "Well . . . yeah . . ." I didn't play it too humble those days. Had to keep the old ego built up.

"Yeah, Kid. You're real good." He cocked his head and let the smoke from his little black cigar curl up alongside his squinted eye. "If you ever need a sponsor . . ."

What he was really saying was he wanted to put some money on me. Lots of money. He had all the right connections to see that the right people used me. He was telling me that if I'd just say the word he'd make me rich. But, as badly as I wanted to become a star, and all that went with it—I didn't want to be "owned" by the mob. And that's exactly what it would have been.

So I just laughed. "Naw . . . but thanks . . ." and just kind of brushed his offer aside. But we both knew that we'd heard each other. Since he hadn't exactly made me a direct offer—though it was clearly inferred—he didn't lose face when I turned him down. But, if he'd made a direct offer . . . well, I don't know what would have happened.

I was working a club in downtown Manhattan, doing about five shows a night. The club had both a lounge and a coffee shop. I worked in the lounge, but usually when I was finished, or between shows, I'd have some cheesecake and coffee. (I guess I was, and still am, hooked on cheesecake. Just a cheesecake junkie.)

Leo, a hot-tempered young mafiosa, who really liked my music, was in the coffee shop too. He had a favorite, called "More." Every time he'd come into the club he'd sit down right in front of me to listen.

Every now and then he'd look up and say, "Hey, Chico . . . do the song." So I'd sing his favorite. Most of the regulars had a special song and they'd give me the high sign when they wanted me to sing it.

I'm sitting there eating my cheesecake. All at once I became aware of Leo and another guy, bald-headed and much bigger than Leo, arguing about something. Their voices got higher and higher. Suddenly Leo jumped to his feet, grabbed a bottle of catsup and smashed it over the guy's head.

I looked up just in time to see catsup running off his head and down his face. It looked like the top of his head was knocked off. He didn't move. Blood, catsup and glass ran down the sides of his head and dripped onto his suit.

The whole place is dead quiet!

Hardly above a whisper—that carried like a shout—he says, "You're dead . . .!"

Leo said something I couldn't hear.

"Ya hear what I said? You're dead! D - e - a - d. Dead!"

Suddenly there's people all over. The assistant, who's an ex-fighter, comes running. Tony, one of the bartenders, leaped right over the bar. They know what's about to happen. They grab Leo and Baldy, separate them and take them out.

Everyone in the coffee shop was just petrified. After a long pause, we all seemed to exhale together . . .

We didn't know what would happen next. But the next night I almost got myself killed finding out. And I didn't even want to be involved, you know.

In those days I had a black leather Angora kidskin coat that I bought from one of the guys (it was probably hotter than a pistol) and wore it all the time. Because of it they used to call me "Rommel the Desert Fox." I guess I really looked like the Gestapo with that black leather coat.

I remember it was raining the following night. I was wearing that coat with the collar turned up around my ears when I got to the club. I always came into the club by way of the coffee shop, through the revolving door. To protect my guitar, I'd hold it next to my chest, back into the door, then turn just as I came out, and leg it through the coffee shop to my dressing room. And . . . I was always late, always in a hurry.

This night I came zipping into the room . . . and when I got my head up and my guitar down, I was half way down the aisle.

Not till then was I aware of the dead silence. It was so quiet that it rang in your ears. Nobody's in the middle of the room. No chairs. No tables. But there's a line up each side of the room. Like two battle lines. Then I realize it's a sit-down because of last night. And right in the middle I come busting in. (That entrance could have cost me my life.)

In a split second I saw it all: Leo on one side of the room with his gang. The bald-head's all wrapped in bandages like a mummy—on the other side with his gang.

And here . . . dressed in black with a guitar case . . . I am. I know I loked like a hit man. Nobody knows what I've got in that guitar case. Every eye in the room is zeroed in on me. I imagine there were lots of itching fingers. Because most of these guys on one side of the room were from the other side of town and didn't know me . . .

All of this came to me in a fraction of a second.

I didn't even slow down in my stride. I didn't dare.

I felt the guys who didn't know me thinking, "You punk, you shouldn't be living anymore . . ."

Sweat was running down my back by the time I got to my dressing room. I collapsed in a chair. The whole thing's funny now. But it wasn't then. *I knew what could have happened.* And it wouldn't have been pretty.

One night I was working in the club Black Velvet in New York. Just a little place, but fixed up pretty plush. Just before I went on the owner came to me. "Hey, Chico," he says, "got some special instructions for ya tonight . . ."

"Okay, Tiny," I said. "It's your orange juice stand . . ."

"It's like this. When we give ya the sign, begin playin' loud—real loud. Wit no breaks. Okay?"

I shrugged. "Okay. It'll drive 'em all out . . ."

"Don't matter. Real loud. Hear me?"

"Yeah. Okay . . ."

I forgot to share this bit of news with my drummer, who's kind of a cocky kid anyway.

So after a while I get the sign. And I gave the drummer the signal. I broke into some real fast numbers with my amp turned up all the way. I finished one and began another . . . without even a pause in between.

I was really working that drummer. He looked at me, his face red, sweat running down his temples. "Whatsa matter wit you, Chico? Ya crazy or sumpin'?"

I grinned back "Hit it! Hit it good!" And went right on.

The kid went crazy. He outdid himself with the cymbals and drums. He grinned his evil grin. "Like that?"

I nodded. He just shook his head . . .

It was so loud all the customers were leaving.

I thought I felt the place shaking. The lights were swinging back and forth. *Just the music,* I thought.

After about forty-five minutes Tiny came down again and gave me the sign to cool it. So we did. Glad to. There wasn't a single customer in the place by then anyway . . .

Sometime later I learned that I'd been the cover-up for a brutal gangland beating. Seems that this kid had rolled a drunk Mafiosa, and stripped him of $800 bucks. So while the drummer and I were slugging it out with the music down below, the boys were "reminding" the kid—with a tape-wrapped bicycle chain—to take it easy on the "family."

When it was over, they cleaned up the half-dead kid, dressed him neatly, and told him to make restitution. They gave him just a couple of days to pay back double what he took. "And if ya don't," they warned, "we might hurt you!"

I never heard what happened after that. But as it was, he came out lucky. Some offenders, for much lesser offenses, had ended up in a garbage can, or in the river with their feet encased in a bucket of concrete.

Moral: don't play around with the Mafia. They play rough.

Before Sally and I met, another incident took place (to her this time) that was later to have a profound effect on our lives. It had to do with a Mafioso chief I'll call Dr. Antonio. He was a real gentleman, very kind and soft-spoken. But he didn't have to speak twice to anybody to get things done . . .

One night just before Sally went on (as I told you before, Sally was a dancer), Dr. Antonio knocked on her dressing-room door and handed her a huge roll of greenbacks.

"What's this for?" she asked.

"We want you to throw the act tonight?"

"You, *what?*"

"We've got a lot of money bet on the act. All ya gotta do is drop one of your batons . . ." (Sally was a three-time world champion baton twirler, had appeared many times on TV, had led the president in parades, given exhibitions at the Rose Bowl, and so on. Now she had turned pro and had a tremendous act.)

She was deeply insulted by his offer.

"I will not!" She shoved the money back into his hands. "Why of all the nerve!"

"Just drop one of . . ."

"I've never done that in my life. And I'm not starting now. Not for you. Not for anybody . . .!" And she slammed the door.

She was really trembling, more from anger than from fear, though she realized the significance of what she'd done. That night she was more careful than before *not* to drop a baton. Dr. Antonio sat near the stage, his black eyes boring into hers whenever she looked his way.

The next night the hat-check girl handed Sally a beautiful sable fur coat.

"That's not mine," Sally said.

"It is now," the girl answered. She motioned to Dr. Antonio's table. "A gift from him . . ."

Sally raged over to Antonio and threw the coat at him. You could have heard a pin drop. In the silence a bartender dropped a piece of ice in a glass. It sounded like an explosion. Everybody jumped.

"Here, take your coat!" Sally said, very firmly. "I don't take gifts from anyone!"

Dr. Antonio didn't say a word. He just sat there. Sally turned on her heel and flounced away. She never had any more offers.

A few nights later Sally was walking down a deserted street to her car. Alone. She had never been afraid in any place. As she walked she became aware that she was being followed. In the darkness she could make out two men. When she stopped they did. When she began walking, they did.

She knew what could—and often did—happen on a dark street. In fact she was in the area where a girl had been stabbed 36 times and raped in full view of hundreds of apartment tenants. And they had done nothing. Nobody had lifted a hand or a voice to help her. (Except for one man who yelled out his window, "Shut up! I'm trying to sleep!")

Sally knew this.

So she boldly faced these two men. When she saw them up close she recognized them. They'd been in the club a few times. She knew they were Antonio's boys.

"Are you following me?" she demanded.

"Yeah.. . ." one of them grunted.

"Well stop it. Go home and leave me alone!"

"We can't . . ."

"You can't? What do you mean?"

"We got our orders."

"Orders? From whom?"

"Can't say. Just orders . . ."

"Orders to do what?"

"To protect you . . . that's what we're doing . . . making sure nuthin' happens to you."

6

Switchblade To Play With

From that moment on Sally had no trouble, no guff of any kind from anybody. And though Sally and Dr. Antonio treated each other with respectful aloofness, they both knew where it was at. So did everybody else. To touch Sally . . . to treat her with disrespect . . . and they'd end up in a garbage can or in the river with a pair of cement shoes—or both.

And who wanted that?

When I came into the picture, I thought that just being Sally's husband would entitle me to certain liberties. I'm still not sure.

One time Sally and I were sitting in a booth at the club with our backs to the door. Dr. Antonio comes in, and we can see him through the mirrors. He's talking to some people as he comes through and doesn't see Sally's old handbag (that looks like a bowling bag) sitting in the aisle. So he knocked it over as he passes by.

I said, "Why don't you pick up your feet . . . you big clumsy—?"

He stopped dead in his tracks. And slowly turned around to look at me. His eyes were just black pools. There was death in those eyes. The guys who were with him, stopped too. All of them just looked at me. I held my breath . . .

All of a sudden he smiles. "Sally . . . Chico . . . how are ya doin'?"

I began breathing again (after making a big mental note never to take such liberties again) . . . and gradually things began moving again in the club. Things were awfully quiet for an instant.

Dr. Antonio seemed to look upon Sally as the epitome of what his mother and sisters were (or might have been). And for some wonderful—but strange—reason he deeply respected her for what she was. After the bankroll and fur coat incidents he never again presumed upon her. He kept her on a pedestal.

Looking back at those days, Sally and I can see God's hand upon her, in fact upon us both. There were times when we could have lost each other. There were pressures and temptations that nobody (except show people) could possibly comprehend. But God gave Sally and I such a love for each other, such mutual respect, that it was evident to others. And they left us alone.

One night in one of the clubs, it seemed that the message hadn't gotten through to all the boys.

We were between shows. Sally and I were in the foyer of the club. It was a long one, with stairs at one end. I had gone up to get Sally some coffee. She was sitting there holding our first baby—Sally Kim—playing with her, talking to her as mothers do. This man came up to her. She had never seen him before.

"What a pretty baby," he said.

Sally just looked up, but didn't say anything. I learned later that she was praying . . .

"Your baby likes toys," he said.

Still Sally didn't say anything.

"I'll give her something to play with." And he pulled out a switchblade knife and popped the blade.

He stuck the point of it right against the baby's throat.

"See, she likes toys . . ."

At that precise moment I started down the stairs. I took in the scene . . . and froze. I saw Sally and the baby sitting there. Also frozen. I didn't know what to do. At that time I didn't know how to pray. I didn't dare yell at the guy, for fear he might kill our baby or Sally.

So I just kept coming down the stairs, the cups of coffee in my hands. Slowly. Carefully . . .

Sally seemed totally peaceful. The whole picture was weird. To this day I'm not sure if that guy ever did see me. He just stood there for what seemed hours. I could hear my heart pounding. But that's all I could hear.

Then, without saying another word, he shifted his eyes from the baby to Sally. She told me later that those eyes were totally expressionless. He stared at her for another eternity . . . then carefully folded up his knife . . . and disappeared out the back door.

In those days Sally and I were working all over the U.S. and Canada. Sally would open the show (having a very high powered act closing with a routine where she twirled a fire baton). I would be back stage holding the baby waiting to go on. My biggest fear was hoping I wouldn't have to go on with a white spot on my shoulder where she spit up or a wet spot . . . but I never did. Praise God. Sally would finish her act and as I was being announced I'd give her the baby saying, "she's wet . . . she's hungry" . . . and I was on.

As our family increased we moved to Detroit and later New York. Sally was modelling at the New York World's Fair and working as a bunny at the Playboy Club while I was trying to get started in the clubs and make some connections with the right agents. The same way wives put their husbands through medical and law school, Sally was doing for me. And after saying no to a lot of offers (because Sally was bringing home the bacon) we started to connect with some good bookings.

It was in New York while working the clubs on the East Side that I started keeping company with the boys. Not that I ever carried a gun (although I admit I did think about it), or robbed a bank. But I was running in the same circles with the guys that did.

There are lots of guys that Sally and I know who are serving time for extortion, murder, grand theft, bank-robbery. And there's also a lot of them that weren't quite that lucky. They wound up in garbage cans . . . or their cars blown up.

And I know a few who walked away from the Mafia. But they're still looking over their shoulder every day. They never know when they're going to be picked up—by either the good guys, or the bad guys.

Before I got to New York I had been running with guys who were involved in things like horse racing, running numbers and stuff like that. But in New York I really began to meet a lot of the big boys. One of them was Sonny . . . probably one of the biggest guys in the city at the time.

He and his boys would make the rounds making collections (for "protection") every week. This included just about every kind of business and store in town, large and small. And I got to know Sonny fairly well . . .

I soon learned that it came in handy—knowing Sonny.

For instance, I was working at a club in Brooklyn called the Palm Room. And one day I got a phone call from the union. This guy said, "We're pulling you off the job at the Palms . . . you didn't file a contract."

I said, "You're crazy! That's all straight."

"We're pulling you out till we get it ironed out."

"Look," I shouted, "there's no problem with that contract!"

I was really fuming. It seems the only thing the union ever did for me was to keep me out of work.

But that was it . . . the union guy hung up on me right in the middle of the conversation.

Just then the owner of the club calls me and really screams. "You no good rat! You bum! What's the idea of messing us up? I'm really gonna fix you. You'll never work here again . . .!"

I rushed down to the union hall and went round

and round with those idiots. But I didn't get any satisfaction at all. Just as I came storming out of there I ran into Sonny—and his lawyer. He always had his lawyer with him.

He often came into the clubs where I would be working. And sometimes we'd have coffee together. He'd say, "Hey, Kid, you sing alright. You're a good kid, ya know?"

I'd nod and sip my coffee.

"If you ever need a good manager, we could probably do some things for you . . ."

And I'd say, "Yeah, yeah . . . I know you guys . . ."

When I came out of the union building that day I was really upset. And, like I said, there was Sonny.

He said, "Hey, Chico . . . how ya doin'?"

At this moment he was under indictment, and I knew that there was probably some guy from the State or Federal Department taking pictures of him from the back of a truck somewhere. And me with him. I looked around to see if I could spot 'em, but I didn't see a thing.

I said, "Not so good. These dudes at the union've got me all messed up!"

"Why? Whatsa matter . . .?"

So I told him.

He listened, nodding his head. Then he said, "Hey, Kid, listen. I know a coupla guys up there that're my friends . . . maybe I can do something for you. I know the guys that run that club, too. I'll call them up and tell them not to be mad at you. It ain't yer fault. Right?"

I said, "Yeah . . . okay . . ." And I thanked him.

Then I grabbed the subway, and in twenty minutes I was home. When I walk in the door the phone was ringing.

It's the union. The guy says, "Mister Holiday (they never called me *mister* before) . . ."

"Yeah . . ." I said.

"Mister Holiday, we just discovered what the error was. And we want you to know it's all straightened out. And you don't have to worry about a thing. It was our fault. We're very sorry . . ."

I said, "Okay . . ." But I still didn't have a job. The Club was still mad at me. And who was going to call them?

So I hung up the phone. Click . . . and it rang again.

"Look, Chico, Baby . . . (It's the Club). Hey, the thing at the union's been cleared up. No hard feelings, ya know? So you can open tonight. Right? Okay . . .?"

I couldn't believe it.

That night at the Club I walked up to the bar and ordered a drink. I said, "How much is it?"

He said, "Forget it. It's on the house . . ."

I said, "Well, thanks . . ."

And he said, "Uh . . . how long ya known Sonny?"

"Hey, we're buddies . . . a long time."

"No kiddin'? Have another drink."

It was really funny.

After that I'd be working at other clubs. I'd be singing and Sonny would come in and sit down at the end of the bar. He'd kind of wave at me, and I'd nod at him. You should have seen the heads turn—

like they're watching a ping-pong match. When I'd finish I'd go over and give him a slug on the arm.

"How ya doin'?"

He'd say, "Okay . . . okay. They treatin' ya okay here?"

I'd say, "Yeah . . ." And if they hadn't been they'd sure enough start treating me right—from that minute on.

One day we got a phone call . . . a voice that sounds like it's just swallowed about ten pounds of ground glass.

The guy says, "Hey, is this here Chico Holiday?"

"Yeah, this is Chico."

"This is Tony." (I knew who he was immediately. It was Tony G, one of the really big men.)

"Hi, Tony," I said.

"Albert and I want ya ta come up and have dinner with us. Tonight. Okay?"

"Yeah, okay."

So Sally and I went. It was a great dinner. Italian spaghetti, wine, the works. These guys looked just like actors in a George Raft movie—green-tinted glasses, slicked-back vaseline hair . . . (Remember, most Mafia don't look like Mafia. Rather than looking like killers with black shirts and white ties, most of them look like bankers, doctors, professional men. (And they are. They really are!)

When we got through eating one of them said, "We like the way you sing . . ."

I said, "Thanks . . ." and looked at Sally. She looked at me. We both knew what was coming.

"Well, Chico . . . if you ever want a manager . . . give us a call. Okay?"

"Yeah, thanks," I said.

For some reason they never put any pressure on me. But I know of a number of people they just walked up to and said, "We're gonna manage you . . ." And that was it. They had no choice. They were literally owned by the mob. They'd tell him what to sing, and when to sing. And that's it.

And if they decided to manage you and you said, "No" and didn't "play it smart"—they had ways to help you change your mind . . . in a hurry.

I know a really good singer who became a cement finisher because of the pressure. And it was years before they'd let him sing. Another singer got shoved through a plate glass window— got his hands and face cut up—because he wouldn't listen, wouldn't take advice . . . wouldn't "play it smart."

7

The Pace Quickens

One day Sally and I were in Chicago—where we'd been appearing at some of the clubs—when we ran desperately low on money. But as luck would have it, we ran into this club owner who'd gypped us out of a lot of money. I had tried to collect from the guy before with no luck. But now we were really hurting.

"Hey, Max . . ." I said.

He tried to look very pressed for time, and began edging away from us. "Uh . . . hi, Chico . . . Sally."

"Max, we're leaving for New York . . ."

He grinned, relieved. "Great. Have a good trip . . ." and he started walking away. "See you."

"Wait a minute, Max. About that money you owe us . . ."

He laughed. "Money? What money? I don't owe you any money."

But he had pressed the wrong button. Like a wildcat, Sally was at him. She backed him up against the wall.

"We need that money, Max. It's ours. And you

cheated us out of it!"

He tried to keep cool. "Look, Sally. That deal's closed. Finished! Now I gotta go. I got an appointment . . ."

Sally didn't speak. She just stared at him.

"Listen, you guys. I'm tryin' my best to be nice. But I'm tellin' ya . . . there ain't no more money! Now get lost! Hear me. Get lost!"

That was too much for Sally. "Look, Max. We need the money. We need it now! And unless you give it to us *right . . . this . . . minute . . .* I'll . . . I'll . . ."

He laughed. "You'll what?"

"I'll call Dr. Antonio."

That hit him. "Dr. Antonio? I don't get it. What's he got to do with . . ."

"He happens to be my uncle. And if you don't . . ."

Max turned as white as a piece of marble and began trembling. He jerked out a roll of bills. "Look, Sally. Can'tcha take a joke? I was just puttin' ya on . . ."

While he was talking, he was peeling off bills. Sally counted. By the time he handed a stack of them to her he looked like he was going to throw up. "There . . . 's that right?"

She counted them again. "Yes. That's right."

Then she gave him the look that means—*look out!* "Don't ever pull anything like that again! Do you hear me?"

"Yeah . . . I hear you. And I won't." He tried to regain his composure, but failed. "Well . . . have a nice trip . . ."

I'm sure it was a long time before Max recovered from that shock.

Not long after we were married, Sally became my manager. She'd been in show business for most of her life and really knew the ropes. She did a better job for us than any manager I'd ever seen. She negotiated contracts with record companies like Decca, Audio Fidelity, Universal International, A & M, and others. We did several records, including one we called "God, Country & My Baby." I helped write it, and think it was a good song. We got quite a bit of publicity when *Time Magazine* printed an article about it being banned on the BBC. (The record went over three quarters of a million.)

It was partly Sally's know-how that helped us go in business with John Molino. John was acquainted with the Mafia and had to literally fight his way out a couple of times. He packed a .38 pistol just for that purpose. We did pretty well with our company which we called Meadowbrook Records.

It was about this time that we decided it would be great if we could get out on the West Coast— because we felt that that's where the real action was. So Sally worked some of her special kind of magic. It was really funny.

She just called up Allan Stanton, the vice president of A & M Records. She said, "Mr. Stanton . . . I'm calling from Detroit. I'll be out there tomorrow. I'd like to have an appointment."

Up till that time I don't think he'd heard much about Chico Holiday. But he did then . . .

Stanton was really uptight. "Are you crazy," he

shouted. "There ain't no way I can see you tomorrow . . ."

"All I need is just a few minutes."

"I can't see you—or anybody—for the next two weeks. And especially tomorrow. Tomorrow's the Grammy Awards. And we're up for five out of six. That's tomorrow night. And there ain't no way that I'm gonna see anybody!"

Unfortunately Mr. Stanton didn't know who he was talking to. He was talking to Sally Holiday. Before he knows what hit him, he found himself saying, "Well, Mrs. Holiday if you're that determined . . . and you want to take a chance on it . . . maybe I can give you ten minutes . . ."

"Thank you very much, Mr. Stanton . . ."

"Remember, I said *maybe*. That's no sure thing. So, if you want to gamble a plane ticket on that . . . it's up to you."

Well, to make a long story short, she got to see Stanton. And they liked the dubs. And they said they'd like to sign me up. But—"Before that," they said, "we'd like to see him . . . so if he could ever get booked in Vegas . . ."

Well, you guessed it. Sally called me from Hollywood and said, "We're going to get booked in Las Vegas . . ."

"But, Sally . . . that's next to impossible . . ."

"I know . . ." she said over the phone.

"It takes a lotta juice. You gotta know people. It's politics."

"I know . . ." she said. Well, you can't argue with a gal like Sally. And I've seen her right so many times . . . but I'm a slow learner.

Well, anyway, we engaged this agent to set up some auditions for me. We gave him about three weeks to get some things lined up, then my drummer and I flew out. (It cost about $2,000 to get there.) As soon as we got in town I met with the agent.

"Well, where do we start?" I asked.

He looked embarassed. "Well, I don't really have anything set up yet . . ."

"You *what!*"

"Well, ya see . . . I wanted to wait till you got here before I really started to do anything . . ."

I couldn't believe what I was hearing.

". . . I didn't know for sure if . . ."

"Well, get on it," I said.

So he started making phone calls. And he starts taking us around to the hillbilly joints. And I mean *joints*. Nothing on the Strip.

"Hey, what is this?" I ask him. "I didn't spend all that money to fly out here to work in some joint in the boondocks!"

He didn't say anything.

"Didn't you work anything on the Strip?"

"Well . . ." he said, "I'm working on that . . ."

I could see right away we'd made a mistake. So here we were. I had no money coming in. And I was paying this drummer.

And Sally was on her way.

Well, I didn't know it then, and wouldn't have recognized it then, but God was answering Sally's prayers. You see, from somewhere along the line she'd gotten acquainted with Jesus years ago as a young girl. And she talked to him. I thought she was weird, but I loved her and she was my wife. I just accepted her the way she was. And (had I known what to look for) I could have seen God's hand at work the day Sally arrived.

It started in the moment the plane set down.

I said, "Sally, this guy blew it. And blew it good."

"What do you mean?" she asked.

"He hasn't done a thing. Nothin'!"

She smiled and said, "Where's the phone?"

I pointed to a pay phone.

She said, "Give me some names."

I gave her a few. She started dialing. Now, I knew Sally. I'd seen her work miracles before. But this was something else. Within an hour she's got auditions lined up—the Riviera, Caesar's Palace and the Flamingo. She didn't fool around.

The next day we drove to the Riviera for our first audition.

And who's working there but Trini Lopez, in the main show room. And that's where the audition is. Man! I looked at it. It must be the biggest stage in the world. It looked like it was 800 miles long, and 300 miles deep, and 500,000 feet high!

Just then I spotted Toni Zoppi. I'd met him in Dallas some years before. I said, "Toni . . . whatcha doin' here?"

He grinned. "I'm with the organization," he said. "I'm doing the PR work for them . . ."

Just then all of the big shots came in. They sat down right in the center of that monstrous place . . . slouched back in their seats and lit their big cigars . . .

Then one of them said, "Okay, Kid. Go through a coupla things."

My drummer was frozen. Everything around us on that huge stage said "Trini Lopez" . . . He'd been entertaining here every night with full orchestra. And here I was with just a drummer and a guitar.

And a busboy was rattling dishes . . .

So I said to the drummer, "Let's do it!"

And I started. I did Malagania and pulled out all the stops.

Pretty soon I notice the entertainment director get up. I see him out of the corner of my eye. He walks up toward the stage. He gave me a cut sign . . . .

I said to myself, *I didn't fly out here all those miles and pay out two thousand bucks just to do two songs and have you say okay!*

I didn't care if I blew it or not. I said to myself, *Mister, you're gonna hear everything I've got to give you!*

The guy stands right in front of me and pounds on the stage. I ignored him.

My drummer doesn't know what to do. But he knew that I'm paying his way, and if he doesn't do what I tell him he'll be walking back to Detroit . . .

By now I'm going into *Granada* . . . and the director is up on the stage jerking on my coat.

"Okay. Okay. *Okay!* You got the job . . .!"

They signed us up for twelve weeks in the lounge, which was great for the first time out.

And you know, it gave me a great deal of pleasure to be able to call up Caesar's Palace and tell them I wouldn't be coming in for an audition. I had a "previous booking . . ."

61

8

On The Way Up

Things were going great now. I was on my way up. We had us a nice house. Driving a Lincoln. Living it up.

Then Sally began bugging me.

"Chico, honey . . ." she would say.

"Yes, Sally . . ."

". . . you need Jesus . . ."

I nodded my head. It had sort of an automatic nod, like those little dogs you see in the back window of cars. You start the car . . . the dog nods. You turn the corner . . . the dog nods. I was that way. Sally would say, ". . . turn to Jesus." My head would nod. Or, "Chico, let's pray about it . . ."

And I had this little switch up by my brain. As soon as I saw that signal in Sally's eye, or she began talking about anything religious . . . then the switch would turn her off.

But my plastic smile would function. And my head would nod. All the time she thought I was listening. *But I wasn't.*

Sally is a wonderful wife. She began praying, "Dear God, don't let Chico hit (really make it big,

real big) . . . till he lets Jesus take over his life."
She knew that if I ever really hit—ever got to the
place with the world in my hands—that it'd then
be too late.

Of course, she was right. But I didn't know it.

Sure, I used to pray in those early days.

But what would I pray?

"Oh, God, let me hit."

"God, let me become a star."

"God, let me become a headliner."

"Let me get my name in lights . . ."

But Chico was at the very center of my world.
Not God . . .

Chico was the part and parcel of my life. All of
it . . .

No wonder God didn't bless my life. There
wasn't room in it for Him.

I didn't need Him. At least not now. That's what
I thought. That's how I lived . . .

Some time before, back in Wisconsin, I'd met
these *very religious brothers*. I liked them. Respected them. And I tried to talk to them about God.
But it seems that they didn't want to talk about
God . . .

I'd say, "Tell me about Jesus . . ."

And they'd parry my question and say, "What's
it like to be in show business . . .?"

"How can I get God to answer my prayers?"
I'd ask.

They would neatly sidestep that one too. "It
must really be great . . . being a successful entertainer . . ."

So I guess I just turned them off. I just concluded that if God's emissaries weren't interested in giving me God's message . . . well, then, maybe God didn't have a word for Chico Holiday. Or maybe I had to work my way into the position where I would be acceptable. So I decided to make it on my own—and become acceptable . . .

But then, I decided to give those brothers one more chance.

While we were still in New York we got a call from one of the brothers. He told us he was coming to the city to visit us. This was a very critical time in our lives. Sally was working as a bunny in the Playboy Club. I was struggling to get recognition. Waiting for that "big break." I didn't know it at the time (and as paradoxical as it seems) Sally was praying (even though she was a Playboy bunny) . . . that God would do something in my life.

You see . . . I was getting so wrapped up in Chico, that I was drifting further and further away from Sally. I was obsessed with success. I was desperately trying to be successful . . .

So this monk came to see us. Just at this time.

When Sally learned he was coming she began to pray all the more. "Oh, Lord, I know this is the time You're going to show Yourself to Chico. This is the time when he will let You into his life . . ."

She got herself up to a high fever pitch of expectancy.

And she got let down. Clear to the bottom.

So he came. Sally was rejoicing. She thought, *He's God's man. He will point Chico in the right direction* . . .

But it didn't turn out that way.

I said to him, "I really need to talk to you about some things in my life. You know . . . how do I know if God's even interested in us . . . ?"

And his answer, "C'mon, Chico. Forget it, man! I'm on vacation. Show me the lights. Show me Broadway . . ."

We asked him to show us The Way.

He wanted us to show him the Great White Way —when I was looking for the real "Great White Way."

Sally thought, *God failed us. He didn't answer our prayers. At least my prayers* . . . She had offered God her life . . . *Take it,* she said, *but please save my husband . . . I can't live without You in our marriage anymore* . . .

At that time our marriage was shaky—I was looking for that big break, for fame. But I wasn't making it. So I asked God's man to help me. He couldn't be bothered. Sally tried to repair the breach —and couldn't. She asked God's man to help us. And he wasn't interested . . .

So Sally tried to commit suicide.

That was one of the most terrible times in our lives. So I decided right then and there that I would make it on my own. Of course I had Sally to help me. But since we couldn't get to God . . . well . . . *let Him go His way . . . and we'd go our own,* I thought.

Sally was different. She recovered. She never did give up on God, even though God's *men* had failed her, had deeply hurt her . . .

So—after this near tragedy, when Sally would talk about the Lord—my defense was up: my head would nod. But as hurt as she had been . . . as impossible as I seemed to be, she didn't give up on me. She was really persistent.

One day in Las Vegas while we were stopped waiting for a light to change—in front of the Sahara Hotel where I was working—Sally said, "Chico, honey . . . we really need to let God take over our lives . . ."

"Yes, Sally . . ." Nod. Nod. Nod. (I had a lot going for me at this time. I was being booked steady on the Strip. I was actually getting to the top!)

"I mean, get to know Jesus . . ."

"Yes, Sally. Yes, Hon . . ." Nod. Nod. Nod.

But finally, for some reason outside myself, she got to me. She somehow short-circuited my "automatic turn-off switch." And I heard her! For a panic-stricken moment, I realized I was vulnerable. And so to protect myself and keep her happy, I tried evasion.

I said, "Sally . . . listen . . . there's one guy I really like . . ."

Her eyes lit up like neon lights. "Who's that?"

"Billy Graham. He's on the right track . . ."

I should have known Sally well enough to know that I'd given her a straw of hope. And I'm telling you, that woman could build a bridge with a straw to begin with.

"Do you mean that, Chico? Really?"

"Yeah, Sally. If Billy Graham would come and sit down with me . . . and tell me about Jesus . . . you know, really level with me . . . then I'd listen . . ."

"And you'd accept Jesus . . . ?"

66

"Well, yeah," I hedged, "you know, if He could answer some of my questions . . . yeah, sure, I'd think about it . . ."

She put on her mysterious Mona Lisa smile and quit talking. And that's really something for Sally. It made me happy, too, because I got her off my back for a while.

What I didn't know, though, when she dropped me off, she went right home to her pen and paper and began a letter:

"Dear Billy Graham: My husband (etc., etc.) . . . So if you'd only come out to Las Vegas, I'm sure he would accept Jesus Christ . . . Please find enclosed a check for a round-trip ticket to Las Vegas from wherever you are . . . Sincerely, Sally Holiday."

Every day after that she beat me to the mailbox. And no matter what mail we got, she was clearly disappointed. I didn't say anything about it for a few days. But after a week or so, she seemed to be getting pretty uptight. Every time a limousine would go by she'd run to the window and peer out . . .

Every time the doorbell would ring she'd jump and answer the door . . .

Something was up. And I was mystified.

One day I was trying to master one of those husband killers called a "Do-It-Yourself-Carpet-Cleaner." The crazy thing was giving me fits. And I had already shampooed a desk, the drapes, two dogs and half a cat . . . when the doorbell rang.

I shut the machine off. "Who'd be ringing at this time of day?" I grumbled, wanting to get the carpet finished.

I opened the door. *And there stood Billy Graham!*

He looked like Billy Graham. He combed his hair like Billy Graham. In fact, he even sounded like Billy Graham. I just stood there, looking like an idiot.

Sally came to the door. "Well, hello, Pastor Miller," she said. "It's nice of you to drop by . . ."

I wondered what was happening. Later I learned that she had met him at a P.T.A. meeting (so had I, but it hadn't "registered"), and had attended a Bible study at his church. She'd told me about that meeting, but my "automatic-turn-off-switch" had tuned her out.

I thought, *how will I ever get rid of that preacher* (though I had to admit he was a real nice guy, and I wasn't really itching to get back to that carpet)?

But Sally was right on the job. "Would you care for a cup of coffee . . .?"

Of course he did.

So we sat down and had coffee. A whole pot of coffee.

And he told us about Jesus. And I listened . . .

I even asked some questions . . .

Like, "Pastor, ya know, there's something that's always bugged me . . ."

"What's that?"

"Well, I believe in God . . . and Jesus . . . but I've always had the idea that God's up there—poised with His big hammer. And when I do wrong . . . then 'bong!' He gets me . . ."

I paused to see if the guy heard me. (You know, too many people "listen" to you but actually don't "hear" you. But this guy heard me. He really heard me. And he let me talk. He encouraged me to talk.

So I did. I got all of my "God-hang-ups" out of my system.)

"Go on," he said.

"Well, if God's like that . . . how can He 'save' a guy?"

"Chico, you've got it all wrong. God isn't waiting up there with His big hammer to get you . . . He loves you . . ."

"He does?" I had to think about that one.

"Yes. He loved you so much, Chico, that He actually sent His only Son—Jesus—to the Cross . . ."

"Wait a minute . . . that's love?"

"That's right. Somebody had to pay the price for your sins . . ."

"And Jesus did *that!* For everybody?" Suddenly a new thought made its way through my brain. Lights began flashing . . .

Pastor Miller saw my expression. "That's right. Not only did He do it for everybody . . . He did it for you . . . Jesus died on the Cross for you . . . *for you!*"

That was too much.

"You mean Jesus—God's Son (this concept really gripped me)—took the rap for me . . .?"

"That's right, Chico. That's exactly right. As you put it, Jesus 'took the rap' for your sins . . ."

This was the first time in my whole life that a clergyman had made sense. I'd had sit-downs with these guys before. *And nothin'!* This guy didn't preach at me. He didn't talk down to me. He didn't press me for a decision . . .

Looking back, I can see that that day, that moment, was when Jesus began moving in (and into) my life. I didn't actually "accept Jesus" as my Savior right then. But, for the very first time in my life, I had "heard" the way to Jesus. The way to Heaven. I knew how to find Jesus. That pastor was so wise. If he had pushed me right then I would have backed off. But he realized I had to let all of this soak for a while.

He knew, somehow, that Jesus had me hooked. *And he was right.*

I know now that I could have simply said, "Jesus, I want You to come into my life . . . to take over . . . to forgive my sins . . . to make me Your child . . ." And He would have done it. *Right then.* My total acceptance of Jesus came a little later. But in a way, as I said, that moment was *the* red-letter moment...

Pastor Miller invited us to his church. And we went. I really felt out of place in a church, but he was an excellent Bible teacher. Before I realized it, I found myself liking the Bible, too. I even found myself reading it some.

Later Sally told about writing to Billy Graham. She told me of the little bitterness that crept into her life when she didn't hear from him. "Before that incident," she said, "I loved Billy Graham. But now, in the hour of my deepest need—for my husband to find Christ—I thought Billy Graham had let me down . . .

"And it wasn't until Chico was singing in the rain at Explo '72 in Dallas that I was able to forgive Billy Graham. I'm sure he never even got my letter. But some day I'll meet him and tell him all about that time . . .

"Anyway," Sally said, "Chico just finished singing . . . and there came Billy Graham. They were on the same platform . . . Billy Graham and Chico talking together . . .

"And I prayed, *Father, forgive me for all that bitterness. You brought Chico to Jesus Your own way. How could I ever have presumed to ask You to send Billy Graham to Las Vegas?*

"It wasn't till then," Sally told me, "that I got peace over the incident. I realized then that God sent a man to Chico who could stay and minister to him for months with love and patience. He was able to spend all the time it took, time that Billy Graham could never have spent . . ."

So it was in Las Vegas where it really all began.

9

Dino's Den

Some of the finest people I ever met in my life have been show business people. Practically without exception, these people have "paid their dues" —they've come up through the ranks, and they've earned their right to success. Of course, like professionals in any given field there are rotten apples. But for the most part, I gladly take my hat off to the entertainers who have made it big. Most of them have dearly paid the price for their "place in the sun."

One man who has especially impressed me is Sammy Davis, Jr. I met him under what I thought (as a relatively new performer) were somewhat "different" circumstances.

I was working at a very posh club in Detroit called the London Chop House, when I got a phone call. A voice said, "I'm Sammy Davis, Jr.'s road manager . . ."

I said, "Yeah . . . yeah . . ."

"That's right," the guy said. "And we're having a going away party for Sammy. It's at the Elmwood

Casino. And Sammy said he'd like for you to come over . . ."

I still didn't believe the guy. So I just said, "Yeah . . . okay . . ."

After he hung up I made a couple of phone calls. And it was for real! When I got over there they had one of the banquet rooms all set up for Sammy's reception. He was just finishing his show in the main room. When he came in everybody rushed right up to him and mobbed him. He'd been working awfully hard (nobody works harder than Sammy) and he was wringing wet. His suit coat was soaked clear through.

I didn't know Sammy except by sight. I wanted to go over and introduce myself, but I didn't want to insult him. Besides, there were all these people hanging around him.

I was talking to another guy when I felt a tap on my shoulder and looked around. "Hello. I'm Sammy Davis, Junior. It's nice of you to come over . . ."

I stammered one of my especially brilliant remarks. He pretended not to notice my confusion and I was grateful.

Some musicians were jamming up on stage. And somebody yells, "Hey, Sammy. Do something!"

He shook his head—no.

I was shocked. Here Sammy had just finished an hour-long show. Maybe longer. And he was really done in. But these idiots persisted. He finally said, "Okay . . ."

He got up and got about eight bars into the song, and a bunch of hookers in the front row began talking and laughing and carrying on. Just ignoring this guy who was pouring out his heart for them. It made me so mad I wanted to go crack their heads together.

When he finished I walked over. I said, "I want to apologize for those people. I really appreciated what you did. Just from watching you . . . just now . . . I learned a lot. How you could go on singing with all those people carrying on is beyond me . . ."

He grinned. "Thank you very much. But here's something I always remember, Chico . . . there's always somebody out there who is listening to you and what you have to say. And I was singing to those people who are listening . . ."

That thought got hold of me. It changed my professional attitude. I remembered it. And years later at Harold's Club in Reno, and in the hotels in Vegas . . . when it was total bedlam . . . and nobody was listening (or it seemed that way) . . . especially when I began to sing about Jesus . . . *then* (because of what I learned that night from Sammy) I realized that there was *always* somebody listening. And I sang for that person.

So now, thanks in great measure to Sammy Davis, Jr., I can sing for that one—the one who needs the love and peace my Jesus can bring—that one person in the crowd who is listening . . .

For a long time these thoughts had only to do with entertaining them. Now I share with listeners the Good News that will change their lives. I used to sing to "help people forget their troubles for a few minutes." Now I sing a message that will "take away their sins and hassles forever."

I praise God that I now have Jesus Christ in my life—that He can and does change lives—and that now with the power of the Holy Spirit singing through me, I have the rare opportunity of bringing a "new life" to every one who is ready to turn in his old one and be born again, anew.

About two years after we moved to Las Vegas, Dean Martin became president of the Riviera. Shortly after that the hotel built a small, intimate lounge that became known as "Dino's Den." It became the "in" spot in town. It was lavishly decorated and gave you the same feeling as one of his TV sets. It was distinctly his . . . and had huge pictures of him all around the room.

It was a tiny place, for only about 50 people. Even the tables were tiny—just large enough for an ashtray and a couple of drinks.

But what it may have lacked in physical size, it made up for in impact and importance. When Dean Martin wasn't there it was quiet. But when Dino came in—which he always did after his last show—the place came alive.

He came there to relax. In fact, it could almost be said that's where he held court. There was no doubt about it, he was the king of "Dino's Den." He was the overpowering personality in that place.

Even though the place was always full of stars, Dino's spirit dominated and permeated the place. Though "Dino's Den" was built for him, in a strange way, *it was him.*

It was sort of the "watering hole." Anybody who was anybody was likely to be at Dino's when Dino himself was in town. Nobody was formally invited to the Den. But they would come. There were guards at the door. If you were recognized on sight, you were in. Otherwise, it would take an act of Congress to get in.

For some reason, I was invited to be one of the first performers in Dino's Den.

I don't know for sure why I was selected. Maybe partly because I was Italian. And since there were so many Italian stars there all the time, it didn't hurt being one.

No matter who was there, or what was happening, when Dino came in . . . everything else stopped. From that moment on it was totally his. That's just the kind of person he is. He didn't demand the attention. He just had it. It was a certain kind of charisma. Whatever you want to call it, Dino had it. He still has. (And I am believing God to reach Dino for Himself, so that all that tremendous talent will be used for Jesus.)

When Dino came in he'd always take the end seat on the settee and give me a high sign. I'd immediately do his song. His favorite was "Dominie" (Tomorrow) . . .

Suddenly, as though somebody had flipped a switch, the place would come to life. Others would hand me requests, and many times as I was singing, different entertainers would come up and do the song with me. It was really like an Italian wedding . . .

One night in particular I remember. It was a mighty impressive lineup. Dean Martin was in his usual place. Johnny Carson was sitting next to him. Then there was Joey Bishop, Brigette Bardotte and

Chuck Connors. Bill Cosby was coming in the door —a huge open archway—when I began one number. And as I was finishing, Vic Damone came in . . . it was pretty much like the "Who's Who in the Entertainment Field."

I'd finished singing one particular number that night. And I was suddenly aware that the room was very quiet. There wasn't a sound. I wondered what was going on . . .

I turned just a little and got the answer.

Standing close enough so I could touch him was *Frank Sinatra.* Just standing there with his arms crossed . . . staring at me with that inscrutable expression on his face that nobody can read. He was just standing there. Like he was evaluating me. Or passing judgment. Or something.

I didn't know what to do, so I just looked back at him. I didn't say anything. I didn't know what to do, or if I should say anything . . .

It seemed that nobody in the Den was even breathing. And it seemed that Frank was hardly aware of it . . .

Finally he said, "That's pretty good, Kid . . . pretty good . . ."

Then he went on talking with somebody else. And I began breathing again. Along with everybody else.

I was just back to the Riviera and Dino's Den is closed. And I bet a lot of people don't even remember it ever being there!

It's funny . . . all that glamour that was there is gone. Some of the stars that came there are dead. At the time I thought what could be greater than this? Well, I can tell you in a word . . . what can and is better than all the glamour, the stars, the excitement—anything the world has to offer—that word is *Jesus*. I thought excitement was to be found in Vegas, New York, R.C.A., United Artist, and television. *But nothing can compare to the excitement to be found in Jesus—and in following Him.*

SILVER DOLLAR
ROOM

CHICO
HOLIDAY

DUSK TO DAWN

Harold's Club, Reno — where Chico first sang about
Jesus. Chico at the Riviera in Las Vegas.

Dino's Den, the Riviera.

Dr. and Allene Wilkerson with Chico and Sally Holiday.

All the Holidays — (back row l. to r.) Sally Kim, Christieve; (front row) Kristen, Darryl, Craig.

Dr. Ralph Wilkerson, Melodyland, congratulates Chico and Sally at Chico's ordination.

Chico and Sally

10

Reno

It was at Reno where God really got to me.

Because of Sally I had gotten exposed to Jesus Christ in Las Vegas. But it was in Reno where He started putting my head on straight.

. . . it was about time for our last little boy to be born—number 5!

We were faced with a couple of problems:

One—I was out of work for a little while. And when you're an entertainer, when the job's finished, so is the money. Cut! Just like that!

Two—I didn't have any insurance to pay for the hospital and doctor. (It's true I had been making good money. Very good, in fact. But it's also true I was driving a Lincoln Continental, and living it up. We were living high, not saving anything. Somehow, the money just went . . . it just simply melted away . . .!)

Then Art, my manager, called me . . .

"Listen, Chico," he said. "I've got something. I've been talking to Roy Powers at Harold's Club . . . and they . . ."

"Harold's Club? Look, Art, I don't want to go to

Harold's! Harrah's is *the* club. Besides, we've got sixteen more weeks at Harrah's as soon as they call me back. And if I go across the street to Harold's . . . it'll blow that booking!"

"Listen, Chico. This is a good thing for you. You'd really do good there."

"Aw, you're crazy!"

"It won't hurt you. You still got Harrah's."

I told him to check it out to be sure. He did and called me right back. "Like I said, Chico. No problem. I checked . . ."

"Okay. But just for a coupla weeks . . ."

It's really strange how things work out. I went there for about two weeks. And stayed there for three months. Then back into another Hughes hotel in Vegas, where I stayed over Christmas and New Year's.

The week after New Year's I went back up to Harold's Club for a couple of weeks. Art said it was to "fill a little hole. And do them a favor. Then you'll come right back to Vegas. And we'll put you in the Frontier for six months . . ."

I said, "Well, alright. That sounds okay."

But it didn't work out that way.

I went to Harold's Club and wound up staying there over a year. It was during that second time at Harold's that I got acquainted with the Sierra Ministries. In fact, that was actually the real beginning of my life for Jesus Christ.

And that episode started the moment I stepped off the plane.

This young kid comes up to me, hands me a tract and said, sort of parrot-like, "Do you know

86

Jesus as your Lord and Savior . . .?"

I said, "Yes, I do." At that time I knew a lot
about Jesus, but I didn't really *know Him.*

The kid, his name was Mike, acted as though
he hadn't heard me. In a way I guess that's not
surprising, because I got off the plane with my
guitar, and I looked like a typical musician. He
followed me, and probably thought I was just
shining it on.

"You really should know Jesus . . ." he went on,
sort of like a recording.

"I know Him," I said.

". . . because He's the only One Who can give
you . . ."

"Hey," I said, "I know Him. I know Jesus . . ."

He just went on and on—like a record. ". . . He
can change your life and make you happy . . ."

By now I was in the main part of the terminal.
And Mike was following me . . . talking a blue
streak. Finally I grabbed him by the arm. "Look,
Brother!" I almost shouted in his ear, "I am saved.
I know Jesus as my Lord and Savior . . ."

He kind of stopped. He looked at me funny.

"I don't know what I can do to prove it to you
. . ." I said.

That stunned him. He was kind of embarrassed.
So while we waited for a cab we talked a little. At
that time I just had a head knowledge of Jesus.
I hadn't yet made that "12-inch step" from my head
to my heart. I didn't have that flowing or warmth.
Like Mike did. At that time I thought "turned on"
Christians like him were kind of weird.

And he thought I was weird.

A few days later I was walking down the street to the Club. It was mid-January. Really cold. I saw this bunch of kids standing out there on the street. They were handing out tracts and witnessing. And they were shivering.

Mike was with them.

"Hey Chico," he said. "Meet some of the brothers and sisters."

He told me their names. I said, "Come on in. Let me buy you some coffee . . ."

They said, "No thanks. We can't right now . . ."

They're all smiles and really nice. And it sort of blew my mind. I could see that they had something I didn't. I said, "Well . . . anytime I can help you, let me know. Okay?"

I hated to leave them out in the cold.

A couple of nights later I was up on the stage singing. Inside Harold's Club. I looked and saw Mike and two of the other kids standing by the door to the Lounge. I had just sung "Brother Love, Salvation Show," and was into "Oh, Happy Day" . . .

Two of the first songs I sang in Harold's that had any sort of a Christian message to them. I finished and came down to where they were. They were standing there shaking their heads.

"We never thought we'd hear songs like that in here . . ."

Mike had a really surprised look on his face. "Yeah . . ." was all he could say.

"Ya see," one of them said, "we were just coming into the coffee shop when . . ."

"When what?" I asked.

"Well, we heard that song about salvation . . .

and we knew it was . . . well, it had to be you . . ."

"Yeah . . . and we just had to come and see . . ."

Mike introduced me to the others. One was Victor, the other was Phil Rothberg, a completed Jew. I began to notice that night that there was a warmth, a love, a straightforward boldness about these kids. And it sort of got to me.

It was the kind of love and boldness that I thought Jesus must have had. They were clearly heirs of the Kingdom. I think some of them were angels. Really, I mean it. *I think they were angels.* Without realizing it at first, I began to get awful hungry for what they had. After I'd been with them, and then left them, I'd feel a void . . . sort of an unfulfilled emptiness . . .

I didn't understand it. But I wanted what they had.

They told us about the Bible studies they were having . . . and about the Sierra Ministries. So Sally and I began attending. We really started getting into the Word . . .

One night after my last show I said, "Phil, you and Dave . . . c'mon. Sally and I'll treat you to something special . . ."

"What's that?" he asked.

"The New Christie Minstrels are over at Harrah's. I'll take you to see them. Then we'll get something to eat." (The New Christie Minstrels were a group of several young people—a very famous folk singing group.)

So poor Phil and Victor were hooked. I mean they were stuck. They were sitting there in all that smoke and booze. And they didn't enjoy themselves at all! I didn't realize it though, at the time. I just knew that they had come into the Lounge at Harold's Club while I was singing . . . so I thought they were used to this sort of atmosphere. What I didn't know, was that all the time they were in the Club (and the primary reason for which they came), they were praying for me all the time, and every time they were there.

As the Christie Minstrels finished their show, they came into the audience and passed out buttons.

One of the gals came up to Phil and handed him a button. And he handed her a tract. "Here, I'll trade you," he said.

She looked very shocked, but managed to say, "Thank you very much . . ." She didn't know what else to do.

After the show we went to eat.

While we were eating, Phil said, "You know, I believe the Lord wants me to go and witness to those kids . . ."

I said, "Well then, you'd better do it right away . . ."

"Why?"

"Because they're closing in a couple of days."

He said—sort of to himself—"Yeah . . . I've really got this burden for them . . ."

The next day he said the same thing. And the next.

So I said, "Well, why don't you go and talk to them."

He grinned. "Okay, I will."

A night or so later he came into the Lounge. And who did he have with him? You're right. It was that girl he'd given the tract to. And a couple of other kids. "Chico," he said, "can we use your dressing room?"

I guess I looked at him kind of funny. He said, "We want to go through some Scripture . . . have a little Bible study . . ."

"Sure," I said, "you know how to get there . . ."

That became a regular routine.

They took her and the others up there and shared Jesus Christ with them. Night after night he'd bring some of the other kids up there . . . and tell them about Jesus. I would be downstairs working. And he'd be upstairs telling somebody about getting right with Jesus Christ. It sort of blew my mind . . .

But after a while I got used to it

Well, in a few days the New Christie Minstrels closed. And Phil left to go back to New York to witness to his parents. They were really strong Jews. When he found Jesus . . . well, they buried him. (They actually had a funeral service, casket and all!) To them their son was dead. So it was really something for him to go back and share Jesus with them.

All of this time I'm getting bolder and bolder. I'm singing more about Jesus than about anything or anybody else.

This wasn't altogether my idea to begin with—it was Sally's.

It went like this: one day she said, "Chico, Honey . . . do you pray and ask the Holy Spirit to sing through you . . . and to take charge—of you—and the entire room when you sing?"

That upset me. "Of course I do!" I said. But it wasn't true. At that time I couldn't even pray at the dinner table. I'd say, "Let the kids do it. It's good for them. They've gotta learn . . ."

Sally told me the Lord would "take over" if I'd let Him.

I resisted. I don't know why. But I felt frustrated . . . really desperate. Because I knew that nothing was "really happening" as I sang. It was still pretty much Chico.

Something else. The devil was talking to me and saying, "Do you *really believe* that stuff . . .?"

But that first night I prayed. Wow! I mean really prayed and asked the Holy Spirit to take over . . . He did! And did He ever!

It was like a hand came down and turned a giant volume control to "off." The room got quiet. And I knew everybody was listening to Jesus speaking to them.

Sometimes I'd forget and race out and start the show—without first asking the Holy Spirit to take over (and that's sort of like a G.I. going into battle —forgetting his rifle, helmet, bullets, bayonet, and all his other equipment, and expecting to win).

Those times, as soon as I remembered, usually during my opening number, I'd immediately . . . I mean right now . . . start praying . . . and down would come the Holy Spirit. And peace would descend upon the room . . . and it was ours.

As a result, things were really happening at Harold's Club. Anybody who came in town would wind up at the Club in the Lounge. It was *the place*. Where the "action is."

The people from the Sierra Ministries would bring all sorts of guests in to see and hear what was happening: Albi Pearson, Dick Mills, David DuPleise, Hal Lindsey, and many others.

Articles began appearing about "Religion Invades Reno" in the local paper. And *Variety*, the trade magazines . . .

Several months passed. I'm still at Harold's. Sometimes I wondered what had happened to the New Christie Minstrels . . . especially the ones Mike and the others were working on.

Then they came back to town.

One night I was in the Lounge doing my second show, when I looked down and see two of the kids from the Minstrels. They were sitting there. Listening. Like they'd never heard anything like this before . . .

After the show I came down. And as I came through the Lounge they were still there. One guy got up and stuck out his hand . . .

"Hi," he said, "I'm Steve."

"Hi, Steve," I said.

" . . . and this is Terry. Hey, Chico . . ."

"Yeah . . ."

"You're a Christian, aren't you?"

"Yeah . . . oh, yeah," I said. "I sure am."

"Well," Steve said, "who do you know who can baptize us?"

11

Do You Need a Skinny Italian Singer?

For about thirty seconds, I guess, I stood there with my mouth wide open.

Then I said, "Wow! Wait right here."

I ran and called Dick Dankworth, of the Sierra Ministries. "Hey, Dick," I said, all out of breath, "I've got two kids from the New Christie Minstrels . . . they want to be baptized . . . now. Right now!"

"Now?"

"Right now!"

"Well, I don't know how we could do it right now . . ." (It was only about 11:00 at night.) He thought a minute. "But, Chico, I tell you what . . . you bring them to the services Sunday. And right after the service we'll baptize them . . ."

So I said, "Okay . . ."

Sunday came. I could hardly wait. Like a kid waiting for Christmas. Steve and Terry went with me to the Sunday services. Right afterwards we went to the home of some friends.

And in their swiming pool we baptized Steve and Terry. It was a precious time.

Later that day, we were talking, when Terry said, "You know . . . the Lord's been talking to me about getting out of the New Christie Minstrels . . ."

I pricked up my ears. To hear somebody talk like that interested me . . . to say the least!

". . . I think I'd like to form another group like it. But we'd sing only Gospel music . . ."

Steve said, "Yeah."

A very interesting thing happened after that. The New Christie Minstrels left Reno. Time went by and I was in Seattle (tell you more about that later).

A friend came up to me. "Hey, Chico," he said, "some gal from your neck of the woods was just named Miss America!"

"Really?"

"Yeah she used to sing with the New Christie Minstrels."

"No kidding?" I really listened then. "What's her name?"

"I don't know. It's in the paper. I'll bring it to you tonight."

He did. *And it was Terry!*

She had sung "How Great Thou Art" in the pageant. Swept the whole crowd off its feet. She was a regular female Billy Graham . . . her singing, and testimony . . .

It really thrilled me . . . to have had a small part in leading her to the Lord. That was really something. And to think the Lord used a skinny Italian singer and a completed Jew to bring Miss America to Jesus. We *are* one in the Spirit!

Back in Reno. Sally and I first went to a Bible study . . . we were just "looking it over." Just sort of casing the place. And we'd been warned about "emotional Christians."

Well this Sunday in Reno at the morning service Sally and I were standing next to Marie, a lovely lady. And while we were singing, she just raised her hands. That's all. But it about freaked us out. We thought she might really get fanatical. You know —roll on the floor and all that. We got pretty jumpy. But we stuck around and nothing happened.

Nothing except . . . these people knew Jesus in a way that we had never known Him. They talked to Him like He was right there. Not just a doctrine or a creed.

They knew Jesus. And we began getting really hungry to know Him like that, too.

The Lord knew all this. He led us . . . very slowly . . . very gently.

It was getting around Easter. Bob and Pat Reynolds invited us to go to church with them in Sparks. He didn't tell us the name of the church. And we didn't think to ask. We didn't know where it was, so we followed Bob and Pat in our car.

For some reason, I was uptight about the whole thing.

"Sally," I said, as we were driving, "what's the name of this church we're going to?"

"I don't know."

"You don't know?"

"No, Honey. I didn't ask him."

"Well, I'll tell you, Sally, if it's one of *those* churches . . . we're splitting!"

"Chico, we can't do that."

"Oh, yes we can. When we drive up to the

church . . . if it's any kind of a Pentacostal Church . . . we're driving right on by . . ."

And would you believe it. When we got to the church, there was a huge banner across the front of the church—"Welcome to our Vacation Bible School." It completely covered the church sign out front! It upset me. But I didn't know what to do about it.

"Let's sit near the door," I told Sally.

"Chico . . ." she pleaded.

"I mean it. I'm not gonna get stuck where I can't get out . . ."

As it turned out, though I was stuck. Being Easter Sunday, the place was jammed. And the usher showed us to *our seats—balcony, front row, center!*

There was no way out. I was fit to be tied.

To make matters worse . . . the associate pastor recognized me. And, you guessed it . . .

Right in the middle of the service he stood up and said—looking right at Sally and me, "Folks, we're very honored this morning . . . Chico Holiday . . ."

I was petrified. Every eye in church turned to us.

". . . Chico's headlining at Harold's Club . . ."

Sally smiled at the people. And I tried to. When all the heads turned back, I said to Sally, "That does it. We're dead!"

She put her hand on my arm. "Chico . . ."

"I don't care. If they start any of that Pentecostal stuff . . . we're gettin' out of here!"

God stepped in just then.

I mean, it was really a service. Elmer Bueno (a missionary from South America) was the speaker and he also sang. Beautifully. Professionally. He had full orchestration on tape, and he sang with that accompaniment. Then he preached. It was Class A, Number One! That guy looked good. He knew what he was saying. He really ministered to me.

I had never heard anything like that. It was thrilling.

He told us that he was from South America, an evangelist.

As soon as I could get to him after the service I grabbed his hand. "Brother," I said, "if you need a skinny Italian singer to go with you down to South America . . . I'm your man!"

Sally looked like she could have fainted.

Elmer Bueno thought I was kidding.

But I wasn't.

I saw him some time after that. "Remember what you said at Sparks?" he said.

"I sure do."

"You really had Sally believing you meant it . . ."

"Brother, I did mean it. If you'd said, 'Let's go!' I would have packed up!"

It about blew his mind.

Shortly after that I was slated to do a concert at UCLA with Hal Lindsey. I got his book, "The Late Great Planet Earth" and read it. It had a tremendous effect upon my life. It cleared away some cobwebs and fuzzy thinking. Some things . . . theological concepts . . . that had been really bugging me, got cleared up. After that we would give that book out at every occasion. We've given Hal's book to Sammy Davis, Jr., Marty Robbins, Dave Madden . . . lots of people who never would pick up a Bible.

I remember talking to Sally about a couple of the things that had bothered both of us. We were walking to Harold's Club one night just before the show. And I said, "Sally . . . I gotta tell you something . . ."

She sensed it was something serious. "Yes . . . Honey . . ."

And I told her. She knew the things that had upset me. ". . . so I've decided to forget it. I'm not going to hassle it anymore. He's my Father . . . and I'm His child . . . and that's all that matters . . ."

Sally smiled at me. "Praise the Lord," she said, "I came to the same conclusion back in Vegas a few days ago . . .

It was great. You know, just to give it over to Jesus. Along with my life . . . and everything.

12

Satan's Woman

Again, God quickened the pace.

The Reno newspaper ran an article that really opened up my world. It was in the Sunday supplement, and the big splash headlines said, "Religion Invades Reno!" Two weeks later *Variety* picked it up and ran it on the front page!

I knew what it took to just get your name in *Variety*. It's the show business Bible. It almost took an act of Congress. Or a heavenly edict to get your name any place in that magazine. And here it was on the front page. In the shape of a cross.

It had my name in quotes all through it, the works!

And *headlines,* no less!

Wow!

It was like God was saying to me, "Look, Chico. You've been paying agents and managers ten percent and more all these years. And what have they done for you? Now I've decided to let people know who you are. That you're singing for me. For Jesus . . ."

A lot of things were happening at that time. Significant things.

Sally and I were about as excited as kids at Christmas.

Because we could see—actually see—God working in our lives . . .

I've got to back up a little to show you what God was doing for Sally. About a year or so before this time I came home for the weekend. We were living in Las Vegas and I was working in Reno. The mail came. I handed Sally some of the mail and I opened some of it.

Suddenly she screamed. And began ripping up a letter. "How dare she! She's a Satan woman . . .!"

"Sally, what's the matter?"

"She's terrible. I hate her!"

Finally I got her calmed down for a minute and she told me the contents of the letter. She had ripped it apart, but the words had burned themselves into her brain.

"Dear Chico," the letter read, "I saw you last week at Harrah's Club in Reno. I was with my husband, so I couldn't talk to you. But I love you. I want to be with you. I must be with you. I'll be in Reno next week. Please come to my room and be with me. I need you. I'll be registered at the Holiday Hotel. My husband and children will be home. I'm leaving them, so I can have an affair with you . . . I'm enclosing my picture so you'll know me . . ."

And I laughed. I thought it was funny.

But Sally didn't think it was funny. She was still M-A-D! And when I laughed it set her off again.

"But, Honey . . ." I said. 'I'm not going to see her . . . or anybody . . ."

"The nerve of her!" Sally shouted. "The demon-possessed nerve of her . . . if I could just get my hands on her . . ."

Even on the way to church that night, Sally was terribly upset and angry. What had happened, apparently, is that the woman had mailed the letter to Harrah's in Reno. I had closed there that same week she'd mailed the letter. So, they had simply forwarded the letter on to me in Vegas. And Sally opened it.

Well, after a while we forgot the incident . . . (at least I did).

Okay, now to bring us up to date again. Here we are in Reno. God is blessing our lives. We're both really rejoicing in Jesus. And I'm singing Christian songs at Harold's Club. Then that woman came back into our lives again. But this time it was much different. The woman wasn't different. Her life was still unhappy and messed up (which I'll tell you about later). But Sally (unbeknown to me) had been praying for her for the past year . . .

Now, let me have Sally tell you about the time she met this woman.

A lot has happened during the past year, and Chico is really deep in the Lord. He's singing at Harold's Club—singing songs about Jesus. One night I walked into the lounge after Chico had started his first show.

And I saw her.

I saw the woman who had written the letter to Chico a year before. The one who had sent her picture. The one who had asked him to have an affair with her. Off and on during the months in

102

between I had been praying for her.

And now as I saw her . . . I was filled with a deep overflowing love for her. She was sitting *alone*. Her eyes were absolutely glued upon Chico. He was oblivious to her. I don't think he even saw her. He didn't even know who she was.

As I was standing there praying for her, a seat opened up next to her. I prayed, *Lord, allow me to witness to her.* Then I sat beside her . . .

I even remembered the woman's name. She looked at me and I said, "Hello . . ."

She looked startled. Apparently she thought I was one of the waitresses. She said "Hello . . ." then turned back to watching my husband.

I just prayed.

Suddenly she turned to me. "I've been here for two days . . . and he won't even look at me . . ."

"Who?" I asked, though I know she meant Chico.

"Him," she said, pointing. "Chico. Chico Holiday." There was an edge to her voice as she said it. A sort of bitterness. And a sort of deep, deep longing.

I didn't say anything.

After a while she sighed. "My husband . . . I'm divorcing him . . . I've got three children . . . I came here for kicks . . . the works . . . and he won't even look at me . . ."

She swung one well-shaped leg back and forth nervously. I realized that she was doing everything in her power to take my husband to bed with her. Yet, Christ's love was flowing through me . . . I felt sorry for her. And I loved her at the same time.

Until the end of the show, she would talk to me now and then. But for the most part, she just sat and chain-smoked. And stared at Chico. As if by the very power of her concentration she could get him to notice her.

But he didn't . . . not at all.

She was literally "hooked" on my husband. A year ago I would have flown into her and torn her apart. Now (thank God) I prayed for her. A year ago I ripped her letter to shreds and threw them on the floor, screaming. Now I was able to share Christ with her . . .

Chico began singing "Bridge Over Troubled Water"—and Barbara began crying.

I touched her arm gently. She started to withdraw, then didn't. She turned to me. "I need him . . . Ch-Ch-ico . . ."

I nodded sympathetically. "Barbara . . . you need someone else even more . . ."

Her eyes opened wide. "You mean my husband . . . and . . . my children . . ."

"Them too. But Someone else."

"Who?"

His name is Jesus . . ."

"Jesus? What can He do for me? I mean . . .?"

"Barbara, Jesus can pull your home together. He can fix your broken heart . . . He can . . ."

She looked at me, half believing, half incredulous . . . for a long moment. Then Chico finished his song. And the spell was broken.

I got her attention only momentarily after that. But I asked the Holy Spirit to speak to her. And He did. A little later, her eyes red, her mascara smudged, she said, "I *know* I need something more . . ." She shrugged and sighed from her very soul.

"But I don't know what it is . . ."

I said nothing.

"Maybe . . . maybe" she said with sudden resolution, "maybe I will go home to my husband . . . and my three children . . . my three babies . . . that is, if they'll have me . . ."

She sat there, swinging her leg, her eyes glued on Chico again. But now and then she'd dig in her purse for a tissue . . .

I didn't say anything more . . . I didn't think I should. Or that I had to. I knew the Holy Spirit was doing all the talking that needed to be done at that moment.

Chico finished his last number.

I knew it would only take him a couple of minutes to change his clothes . . . then to come charging down the stairs . . . and to meet me. To go home. Or out for coffee . . .

Then, there he was, threading his way between the tables.

Beside me, I both heard and felt Barbara's quick intake of breath. And I felt a deep sadness for this poor deluded woman . . . knowing the shock she would soon receive—as she now learned the truth about Chico. And about me.

He came up to me. "Hi, Hon . . ." he said. And I felt her reaction. Jealousy. Anger.

I took his hand. "Chico. I'd like you to meet my friend . . ."

He said, "Hi." Then turned back to me. "When are we going to eat? I'm starved."

I didn't know what to do. I wanted to continue sharing Jesus with Barbara. Chico wanted to eat. *Lord, help me,* I prayed. Chico started talking to a friend near the door waiting for me to finish talking to my "new friend."

"Barbara," I said. "All the time Chico's been singing I've been praying for you . . ."

Her eyes went wide. "Praying for me . . .?"

"Yes. Chico's been singing about Jesus . . . about love and peace . . . about how your life can be filled with happiness . . ."

She looked puzzled. "I heard what he's been singing . . . but . . . I don't understand. Why have you been praying for me?"

"Because you've been telling me about your home breaking up . . . about how lonely you are . . . about how you want something new and exciting in your life . . ."

Chico came back looking at his watch. He didn't know the struggle that was going on. "Sally . . ."

"Just a minute . . . Chico's a good man. But even he can't make you happy . . ."

She bristled at that. I ignored it.

"Only Jesus in your life can do what needs to be done . . ."

She looked at Chico. Then at me. A faint awareness began to dawn . . .

". . . Chico's happy in Jesus. And so am I. We'd like to take you to dinner and tell you about it . . ."

She put her hand to her mouth. Her face went pale. "You . . . and, and . . . Chico . . ."

I nodded. "Yes. My name is Sally. Sally Holiday. Why don't you come with us . . . and let us show you how you can find . . ."

That's as far as I got. With a great, painful sob she rushed out of the room. Out of the Club. And —till this time—out of our lives. I pray that God will allow us to meet her again. So we can lead her to our Savior . . .

*   *   *

Sally was pretty upset about that incident. So was I for that matter. Because we both felt that we had failed to reach this woman for Jesus. But Sally tried. I had nothing to do with it. Though, in a way I feel responsible. Because I sang to her about Jesus many times (according to what she told Sally), but I didn't reach her. . . . We learned later, thank God, that Barbara did go back to her husband and three children. Maybe when she reads this book she'll come to Jesus . . .

Some interesting things, some of them really heavy and some funny, took place while I was in Reno. I'll share some of them with you in the next chapter.

13

Church at Harold's Club

I walked a lot while I was in Reno. I walked through most of that city on my time off.

You see, Sally and the kids were in Las Vegas most of the time I was there. I'd finish the show—usually about two or three in the morning—and all there was to do then was to go to my room.

Or to sit in the Lounge and drink coffee. Or gamble. And after I found Jesus none of that other stuff appealed to me.

So I began putting together car models. And ship models. I had my whole room looking like some kind of museum. To this day I can't stand to look at one of those boxes on the shelves of a toy store.

But this particular morning I drank coffee as long as I could stand it. Then I went to my room to put some more models together. Though I was tired and bleary-eyed from working all night, I didn't want to go to bed yet. I got all my stuff out, reached for the tube of glue. And the tube was empty.

"Man! What'll I do now?" I looked at my watch. It was early, but if I took my time walking I could get down to Woolworth's just about the time they opened. So I set out . . .

I got there just as the doors opened.

When I walked in I met this old clerk. She gave me a funny look. She apparently wasn't pleased with what she saw. Nobody else was around . . . so she came up—but not too close—and said, "Can I help you, Sonny . . .?"

I ignored that description. "Yes . . . I'd like a coupla tubes of airplane glue . . ."

That set her off.

Now I was obviously everything she had thought I was, and more. I could almost hear the wheels go around in her head. She did a double take . . .

"Oh, no you don't, Sonny . . . not from this store . . ."

"Whataya mean . . . I just want some glue . . ."

"I know what you want. I know what you want it for, too. You want to get high on it again. For sniffin'!"

"Look, Lady," I said, with all the patience I could muster, "I just got off work. And I'm building these airplane models . . ."

She cackled. " 'S what they all say. But they don't fool me one bit. You don't either, Sonny . . ."

"Look," I said, "I'm tired. I want to buy some glue. Are you gonna sell it to me? Or not?"

She tightened her crusader lips. "Sure I'll sell it to you . . ."

I sighed. "Okay, then. Just two tubes . . ."

"I'm not through yet. I'll sell it to you . . . if you

bring your mother in here with you."

I was aghast. "My mother? My mother! Look, Lady . . . I'm married. I've got five children. I'm grown up . . ."

She crossed her arms self-righteously. "Your mother . . . or no glue. It's up to you . . ."

I made one more stab at it. "Lady . . . my mother's been dead for two years . . . I don't have a mother. But I do have a wife . . . and five children!" I held up five fingers. "Five children!"

She would not be moved.

"Sorry, Sonny. No mother. No glue. And that's final!"

I was fit to be tied. But that was it. I didn't get any glue from Woolworth's.

One night while I was singing there in Harold's, a bunch of Christian brothers and sisters came in. Albi Pearson and Andre Crouch were among them. (Needless to say, we really had church that night.) They came in as a group and filled the Lounge. I could see the cocktail waitress from where I stood. It'd been a rather slow night . . . and now she apparently thought she'd make a killing in tips. So she got her pencil and made the rounds . . .

I could see her shaking her head.

Meanwhile, the bartender was getting setups all ready. He got a bunch of glasses ready. Iced up. Everything was right at his finger tips. Then she came back with the orders . . .

"Three Seven-Ups and an orange juice."

"Come on. Come on. Give me the order."

"That's it. That's the order."

I knew what was going on, though I couldn't

hear it. It was about all I could do to finish my song.

The bartender's whole body showed unbelief. I could hear what he had to say—even above my music . . .

"Ya *gotta* be kidding!"

"No. That's the whole order . . ."

He was shaking his head as he filled the order.

The next night when I came to work, the waitress was waiting for me. "Were those your friends last night, Chico?"

I grinned, expecting an explosion. "Yep. They were my friends."

She looked me right in the eye. "Chico . . . ya know, I never enjoyed serving people like I did those last night . . ."

"What do you mean?"

"I don't know, really." She shrugged. "But I felt so good around them. So clean. I just felt like they loved me. Ya know what I mean . . .?"

I nodded. "Yeah, I know. I know what you mean."

During this time, God was setting me up for serving Him. At that time I didn't know too much about minding God . . . I mean, about finding His will for my life. I just sort of stumbled along, with His hands guiding me. And somehow, He blessed the songs I sang—my "ministry"—I guess you can really call it.

That's actually what is was. Though I thought I was doing my own thing in Harold's Club, scores of people were influenced. I wasn't aware of this, of course. Praise God!

Quite often a little old lady would come up to me after the show, or while I was on break. With her low-cut dress and tinted hair . . . and too often, slurred speech . . . makeup streaked from crying . . .

And say . . . "God bless you, Chico. You remind me of my son. He's about your age . . ."

Or, "That song reminds me of revival meetings I used to go to . . ."

Or, "I'm going back home . . . try to find God again . . . and go back to church . . ."

Looking back, it seems incredible that God would reach down and touch the lonely, sinful lives of people . . . in a gambling house.

But then, maybe that's not so surprising. He came to reach the ones that nobody else was reaching . . . to minister to the sick, to heal the leper, to open eyes and heal hearts.

The pastor of the church in Sparks, the one Sally and I went to on Easter Sunday, wrote a note to the pastor of Trinity Temple in Las Vegas. In the letter he told Pastor Sharp what I was doing. So later, when Sharp came up to Reno, Pastor Bob Willis said, "You've got to go see this guy at Harold's Club!"

"You mean Chico Holiday? The one you wrote me about?"

"That's the one. He's singing Gospel songs . . . Jesus songs . . . right there from behind the bar, on the stage."

'You're kidding!"

"No. He really is."

So they both came to Harold's Club on a Tuesday night. But that was my night off and I didn't get to see him then. But he left a note. "If you ever come to Vegas, I'd like to talk to you. And have you on our television show . . ."

Looking back now, it seems that that was the hook God used to get me started in serving Him outside the entertainment circuit . . . I'm glad Bill Sharp wrote that note.

In Las Vegas, we heard that Elmer Bueno was at Trinity Temple. I said to Sally, "Hey, let's go."

So we went.

14

God's Minister of Maintenance

Las Vegas's a difficult place to minister. And
Trinity's youth groups were dwindling. Sally and I
went there one Sunday after we got back from
Reno, and met the pastor of Trinity Temple, and
he asked me to sing some Sunday. And I did—he
then said, "How about coming in on a Wednesday
. . . and doing a whole evening for our youth?"

I said, "Okay."

Well, that first night there were about 85 kids
there. A lot of them were right off the streets. Of
course some had been there before. But scores of
them didn't know anything about Jesus or who He
was.

The whole night was a blessing to all of us.

I guess some of the kids later went to the pastor
and asked him if we could come again. He asked
me and I said, "Sure."

"Next week?"

"O.K."

Meanwhile, I had signed a contract to do my first "Christian Album." We had planned to do it live at Harold's Club. The Lord closed the doors on that so we started cutting in Las Vegas at United Sound. We had blocked out three weeks for the session so we had all the time we needed . . . time the Lord provided to spend with the kids coming to us for guidance and love.

Well, after a few weeks, the pastor said, "Chico, we've got an office here if you want to use it . . . you know, to work with some of the kids during the week . . ."

I said, "Okay . . ."

And that's actually how the transition took place.

The Wednesday night youth group grew. 85 to 120 . . . to 200 . . . to 300. It was thrilling to see them come in. At first they came in totally raw and rough. A lot of them dressed in jeans and sandals. Most of them had never touched a Bible. Or heard about being born again . . . or being filled with the Holy Spirit.

But they began changing.

Wednesdays became victorious times.

Scores . . . came to Jesus Christ. Praise the Lord! Praise God!

Well one thing led to another. Then one day the pastor called me into his office.

"Chico . . ." he began, "I hardly know how to say this . . ."

"Just say it," I said.

"Well, we need you here. On a full-time basis." He looked a little embarrassed.

I guess I was sort of expecting that. "Well . . ."

"Well . . . all we can pay you is fifty dollars a week . . ."

I thought about that for a minute. I'd been making a lot more than that. A *lot* more. But this was something different. This was singing for Jesus. This was seeing lives changed. It was actually working in partnership with Jesus. He had done a lot for me. And for Sally. And our family . . . (I knew with five kids and Sally and I that fifty dollars a week would hardly take care of us, but we knew Jesus and we knew that He would!)

I said, "I'll take it."

With that simple statement, I entered into another school of ministry . . . and suffering.

I ministered to the youth . . . and they to me . . .

(Later I learned we also ministered to the adults, but I didn't realize that.)

But, in ways I never dreamed, I was being ministered to . . . I was being shaped . . . refined . . . (and when I say I, I mean both Sally and myself) fashioned into the likeness of the One Who had called us.

In some ways these months in our lives were glorious.

In some ways they were freeing and exciting.

In other ways they were frustrating.

. . . and as the rough edges were being chipped and sanded away . . . it hurt. It really hurt.

I remember some of those days.

I would come into the sanctuary of Trinity . . . confused . . out of my depth . . . and I would cry. *"Lord, what are You doing with me? What are you trying to show us? Oh, God, please help me . . ."*

And that's when I got to know the "saint of the sanctuary" . . . Trinity Temple's "minister of maintenance"—Brother Mel—who had pastored a number of churches, all his life, in fact.

This young man is past seventy . . .

But he's younger in spirit than anybody I know.

And somehow he was always there when I needed him.

I remember walking into the sanctuary one day, upset and confused.

And there he was. He looked like Friar Tuck.

Short, heavy set. Big smile. (He always wore a baseball cap, which I don't think Friar Tuck ever did.) And the people loved him. Especially the kids. If you wanted to see a full house—just announce that Brother Mel was going to have a Bible Study. They'd come out of the woodwork . . .

This particular day, Brother Mel was there. Praise God!

And this is how it happened . . .

I was sitting here, strumming my guitar, singing quietly, kind of praying, kind of trying to get my head together. You've probably done the same thing. Maybe not with a guitar. But . . . well, you know.

The door opened and he came in. At first I wasn't even aware that he was there. Then all at once he slapped me on the back. "Chico, you long-legged Dago! How are you, Brother?"

"Hi, Beelzebub?"

That was it. Our friendly, loving, insulting, brotherly greeting. But it meant a lot to both of us. Especially to me.

Then he was at it . . . vacuuming, or dusting, or picking up, or whatever.

This day, I laid down my guitar and followed him around. Just chatting. Just saying things to keep close to this saint. And he answered . . . knowing there was more. But very wisely not getting serious. Letting me take the lead.

Finally I said, "Brother Mel . . ." (That was the signal: *when I called him Brother.*) His ears perked up—his radar had gotten the message.

"Yes, Chico . . ." He kept right on doing what he was doing, but his antennae were quivering.

". . . how can I know God's will for sure?"

He just looked at me. He knew there was more. And there was . . .

"You know, . . . in show business I was making lots of money . . . and now, well . . . (I paused, a trifle embarrassed, but his helpful silence urged me to go on, to open up.) Well, what I mean is, I used to pay my agent five times a week over what I'm making here at Trinity . . ."

He kept pushing the vacuum cleaner. I kept following. He nodded and I knew he was not just listening. *He was hearing me.* And what a difference there can be between those two.

"What I mean is some people have been telling me that since I'm not earning big money on the Strip . . . you know, like I did . . . and still can . . . well, they say I'm not taking care of my family, my responsibilities right . . . know what I mean?"

He just nodded.

"Well, what I'm trying to say . . . what do you say? What do you think the Lord's saying to me?

I mean . . ."

That's all I could say. Remember, I was a brand new child of God. I had no deep grounding in the Word. I needed help . . . and I had come to the right place. That precious brother said, "Well, Chico, let's just see what God is saying to us—right now—in his Word . . ."

And he'd open up that old Bible of his (though he really didn't have to open it, he could have quoted hundreds, or even more, promises from his beloved Book) and squint a little as he thumbed its well-worn and marked pages.

He'd find the place he was looking for (it didn't take long), and say, "Well, Brother, here's what God is saying . . ." *And he'd read from God's Word.* Just to hear that man read was a benediction. He wouldn't say much afterwards. Just enough. Right on target . . . because the Holy Spirit had set his sights right on to my deep need of the moment . . .

Then he'd put his big old hand on my shoulder and pray for me . . . I can feel it there right now. How I praise God for that man. I hope he knows how much I love him. And, you know, I believe he does. He's just that kind of a guy.

God knew what He was doing when He sent Sally and me to Trinity Temple in Las Vegas. Because it's there that God put us through the furnace of both blessing and affliction. It's there that we learned to put our absolute trust in Him.

And it was there that we learned the bittersweet agony-blessing that comes when God's children walk in the light.

Part of that agony-blessing came as God gently separated us from a number of material things that we had come to treasure. And to depend upon.

Part of the agony-blessing came through the Kellies . . .

15

Kellie the Hellion

She was just that, a hellion.
A wild filly.
I think we first met at one of the youth rallies.
She was beautiful.

And she knew it. She'd walk down the aisles—hips swinging—usually late. Flipping her pony tail from side to side. Watching the reactions. The looks in the eyes of the boys. And the men. And the women.

Sally was drawn to her instantly.

I was too . . . in a way. But later I got so I could hardly stand her. More about that later.

Kellie was in high school at the time. But for her school was a necessary evil. Also, a place to get hold of drugs. She had tried them all. In fact, she was quite knowledgeable about everything. Everything . . .

Not just the "fun things" of sin. She was involved in crime. The rackets. Though at first I doubt that she had any idea what she was getting into.

The thing that finally turned her to Jesus was this guy. Not him, really. But the way he treated her.

He was a real swinger.

He was more than that, though. He was involved in white slavery (prostitution). And drugs. A big pusher. He was near the top. And involved in making deals for drugs. Locally and internationally. He'd deposit the money, personally, in the Swiss banks. He was really into it.

And Kellie was his girl. Even though she was only fifteen at the time. She was built like a mature woman.

For some reason Kellie fell in love with this guy, I'll call him Larry. Larry liked her, evidently. But he was using her. And wanting to train her to be a high class prostitute.

(There's a lot of that in Las Vegas and Reno and cities of that type.)

They keep the girls on reds, which enhances the sex drive. At first the girls like the whole swinging scene. The excitement. The big money. The travel. The different well-known men. Big stars and entertainers. The whole trip.

Then, of course, they're hooked. Into the system. Into the drugs. And can't get out. The only way out is in a plastic bag out in the desert. It happens! It happened to one of Kellie's friends. I think that was about the time she started coming to our rallies at Trinity . . .

But even though she was scared, she wasn't ready to give it all up. She thought she was above the cheap tawdry part of it all. But of course, she wasn't. Nobody was.

She'd come to church a few times. She'd even made a profession of knowing Christ. But it was apparently just for show. Then she'd come hip-swaying down the aisle, raising her hands and shouting at the top of her lungs, "Praise the Lord! Hallelujah!"

She made such a display of herself . . . and all, that Sally would walk right behind her down the aisle trying to hide some of her sensuality.

I think that's what really turned me off of Kellie. It turned a lot of others off, too.

Kellie loved Sally. And Sally Kellie. Because of that Kellie was at our house a lot. Too much, I thought. A long time later—when Kellie really came to Jesus—she confessed to Sally that she had had a crush on me. She cried about it and asked forgiveness, but of course Sally had forgiven her before she even asked.

I know now that Kellie desperately needed male approval. She needed me as sort of a father figure. I didn't know that then. And she used to get on my nerves.

She got on the nerves of lots of the people at church, too. They'd come to me and say, "I think Sally's crazy to put up with Kellie . . ."

Or, "Kellie comes to church just for show . . ."

And, "Kellie doesn't plan to let Jesus take over her life. She comes here just to attract the boys . . ."

And, most of that was true.

Till the night Kellie came to our place. Crying. Desperately upset.

"Why, Kellie . . ." Sally said, taking her into her arms.

Even I was concerned for the girl. She was near hysteria. Her eyes were wide. Like a frightened animal's.

We tried to calm her down. But she sobbed convulsively for an hour or so. After a while Sally said, "Honey, do you want to talk about it . . .?"

Kellie bit her lip. All the color was drained from her face. I knew this was no show. Something had really gotten to Kellie . . .

Sally talked soothingly to the girl—so worldly-wise, and yet still such a child—for several minutes before she responded. Then she sighed deeply and nodded.

"Do you . . . do you . . . re-remember Shirley?"

Yes . . . we remembered. She'd come to the rallies a few times with Kellie. She, too, had gotten hooked into the system, in the same ways that Kellie had. A lovely girl. But hard. And unreachable. She'd apparently gone too far for the love of Christ to penetrate her blown-out mind.

Kellie put her face in her hands and shuddered. She looked up. A veritable picture of tragedy. "They found Shirley today. Out in the desert north of town . . . in . . . in a plastic bag . . . she'd been dead . . . d-dead for several days . . ."

Sally and I looked at each other. We knew what it meant. Shirley had just known too much. They had to get rid of her.

"Do you know who did it?" Sally asked.

Kellie nodded. "Yes . . ."

"Do they suspect that you know this?"

She nodded again. "I faced him with it this afternoon. I faced him with the whole thing. The drugs. The girls. The trips to Switzerland . . . I know, because I was with him . . ."

"What'd he say?"

"At first he got very angry. Then he tried to sweet talk me. I could see it in his eyes . . ."

"You could see what in his eyes?" Sally asked.

"That I'd gone too far. I mean . . . I mean . . ." She shuddered. "I mean, I think I'm going to be next . . ."

She turned her lovely child's eyes to me. "Chico . . . I know I've given you and Sally a sort of bad time. But I'm different now. I mean . . . I know now what it's all about . . ."

Sally said, "We love you Kellie . . ."

"I'm not through yet. What I'm trying to say is . . . will you help me? I can't go back home. I've got to get away someplace . . ." her voice trailed off.

Sally said, "We've got just the place . . . the Home of the Good Shepherd . . ."

"The Catholic Home?" Kellie asked.

"Yes, Honey. The nuns are beautiful. They'll take good care of you . . ."

And that's where we took Kellie—along with a number of other girls who'd gotten all mixed up. The Mother Superior there is a saint of God. She really knows Jesus Christ personally. And she's totally filled with and possessed by the Holy Spirit. Walking into that place is like walking into the presence of Jesus Himself . . .

Now, after a few years, Kellie has grown to be a rather fantastic young woman. She was given a scholarship to go to a Christian college. She accepted it, but chose to spend a few more months at the Good Shepherd . . . "So I can minister to some of the girls."

I praise God that He let us minister to scores and scores of young girls—and young men—who'd gotten so mixed up, and their lives so torn up, that nobody, nothing could ever have straightened them out . . . except Jesus. *And He did.*

Sally really ministers to those girls. And I'd like to have her tell you a little bit how it all started.

Well, as Chico has already told you, I was three times a world champion baton twirler . . . about all my life, it seems. As a very young girl I won trophies and championships with my twirling. I led parades for the President and others, featured in half-times at football games, the Rose Bowl, traveled with the USO overseas. Night clubs. T.V., movies, the works.

And then Chico and I got married; I'd appear at the same clubs where he was singing. We were a sort of a team. Only we didn't bill ourselves as husband and wife. Somehow, married teams don't always click. Some do. But we didn't bill that way.

At a rather crucial place in Chico's career I decided to get a job at the Playboy Club to help pay the bills.

This sounds rather strange, and I don't understand it myself, but God kept watch over me in the Club. In a very limited way I knew Jesus at that time. I never smoked or drank. And I never dated, or even thought about any of the men . . . never. Even before Chico and I met, I never dated men from the clubs I played.

The only Scripture I knew was John 3:16 . . . and I'd quote it to myself frequently. I know it sounds crazy. But that's the way it was.

I'd see a man with a woman who was obviously not his wife. And I'd pray for him. *Jesus, don't let their lives be ruined. Let them get back with their own mates. Please, Jesus.*

Or when I'd learn of girls who got in trouble, I'd pray, *Jesus, please help them. Show yourself to them . . .*

Anyway, God has tremendously used this phase in my life to His glory. Like in Kellie's case. I think I was about the only woman who could ever have ministered to her. Once when Kellie was trying to pray at the altar of the Trinity Temple, I knelt beside her.

"Kellie, Honey . . ." I said. "Jesus can protect you. He can get you out of the mess you're in . . ."

She flipped her ponytail impatiently. "Sally . . . you just don't understand . . ."

"I don't understand what?"

"You just don't understand what it's like . . . you know, the clubs . . . the men . . . the attention . . . you know, the way they look at you. I mean . . . well, you just don't understand. Nobody does . . ."

Then I whispered. "Kellie . . . I do understand . . . you see, I was a Playboy bunny . . ."

Her eyes opened wide. She hugged me convulsively. "Oh, Sally . . . somebody understands! Oh, praise God. Somebody finally understands. You *do* understand!"

Scores of times God has allowed me to minister to women in a way that nobody else had been able to minister—simply because of that chapter in my life. At the time I was a bunny I didn't know what God was preparing me for. Now I do.

And I praise God for the way He has led . . .

God has also given me compassion—empathy, really—for all sorts of women. Even prostitutes. *Perhaps especially prostitutes.* God has also given me a burden to reach them with Jesus' love.

I don't really understand why so many women—Christian women included—are so fearful and defensive about prostitutes. Unless it's because of fear . . . fear that their own husbands will become involved with them. There's more than that, though. It seems to be an unfounded, hysterical sort of feeling. More an emotion than a logic.

But I love them. I really love them. And God has allowed my life to touch many of them. Through this I've made a great discovery: Jesus loves prostitutes too. He loves them exactly as He loves any other kind of lost, alone sinners . . .

Of course the New Testament shows us His love for them. But somehow prostitutes are so low down on our scale of sins that the average church would be scandalized if one of "them" so much as entered the doors.

Once in Reno a woman came to me and asked me to sign a petition to close down the houses of prostituition. In fact, she came to me during a church service.

She waved the petition in front of me and said, "Sally, you've got to help close down those evil places . . ."

I don't disagree. They should be closed. But she was actually raving and ranting . . . her attitude upset me.

"Mrs. Fisher," I said, "have you ever taken Christ to them?"

It was like I'd struck her.

She turned pale. Her hand flew to her mouth. "What do you mean . . .?"

"I mean those girls need Jesus. Most of those girls are in total bondage . . ."

She looked like she was about to faint. The petition was forgotten . . .

"Mrs. Fisher, I know that many of them love their world with Satan. But others want out. They want help. They are weeping and crying, 'Help me!' But they know they are trapped. They know that thousands of women hate them . . . and will never help them get free . . ."

Mrs. Fisher's eyes were as round as dollars, filled with something akin to horror. She tried to talk a time or two, but couldn't get any words out.

I went on. "I don't think we're ever going to close those houses of prostitution . . . except by going in there and sharing Jesus with those hopeless women . . ."

"But . . . but . . . how could we?"

"What do you mean?" I asked.

"They won't let us in?"

"Mrs. Fisher," I said, "they can't stop us. If we go in the power of Jesus we can get in. I'll go with you . . . we'll go together. And we'll tell those women that Jesus loves them . . . and that we love them . . ."

She was totally bewildered. "I . . . I'll have . . . I'll have to think about it . . ." She stuffed the petition in her purse and walked away, or rather, stumbled away. She was really confused and upset.

But God has given me a compassion, as I said

before, a real empathy for unfortunate women. I've been able to go into female prisons to share Jesus. It was hard. The hardest place I've ever been. Nothing I said seemed to make any sort of impact.

After a while all I could do was stand there and weep. I hope we sowed some seed. Because I know we seemed not to even come close to touching any of those women . . .

So you see, all of this had a bearing on my deep, deep love and concern for Kellie. I love her as much as I love my own children. Now when I see her . . . it's so precious. She's so beautiful. So lovely. So aglow with the Spirit of God.

I thank God He allowed Chico and I to become involved with her broken . . . her hopeless . . . her dead-end life . . .

16

Superstar

A couple of things happened in Las Vegas that had a direct bearing on where we are now. I don't necessarily mean geographically. But that, too.

One was when Sid Colan handed us the world on a platter . . .

Sid's a promoter. He's either got lots of money, or he can get his hands on it. He had made a number of really big stars. Not all of them, in my humble opinion, are really stars. But money, the right connections, the right exposure—stuff like that—was what "made" them.

We had just started at Trinity Temple and one day I got a call from Sid. I had known him for some time. But we weren't exactly buddy-buddy.

"Hi, Chico," he said. "This is Sid Colan . . ."

"Oh, hi, Sid."

"Chico, I'd like to talk to you and Sally very seriously about your careers . . . and things that I'd like to do . . ."

While he was talking, my head was spinning. I knew very well what a man like Sid could do. So,

in the few seconds he was speaking, I was thinking
. . . and praying . . . *Lord, help us to know what
to do* . . .

". . . so, could you and Sally have lunch with me
at Caesar's?"

"Sure, Sid." And we set the date.

He got right to the point. We'd hardly sipped
our coffee before Sid said, "I'd like to make you a
star . . ."

Before that really had time to soak in he said,
". . . I don't mean just a star. I mean a super star
. . ." And he named one he had just pyramided to
super-stardom.

Sally and I were new Christians, remember. For
years we had aspired to this place. We had paid our
dues, so to speak. We had worked . . . and fought
. . . and clawed our way to the top. Or almost the
top. And now that we knew Jesus . . . here's this
really fantastic offer.

It was truly the sort of offer that scores of entertainers would literally have sold their souls for.

Now we sat there . . . scarcely able to breath.
But both of us were praying. I said under my breath,
Lord, help us . . . that's all I knew how to pray.

"We believe that you've got everything that's
needed. You've certainly got the talent . . . the vocal
ability . . . you know how to handle yourself. You've
been in the business long enough so you won't be
dazzled by what the business really is . . ."

Sally squeezed my hand and I knew she was
praying. But neither of us spoke at this point.

"In essence, though, I'll be merchandising you
like a package of cigarettes or a bar of soap . . ."

I knew that was true, but I appreciated him leveling with us. I took a deep breath. "What do you have in mind . . .?"

He sipped his drink. "Well, Chico, what we would like to do is dump the image you've got right now . . . give you a different name . . . different identity . . . we'd pull you off the scene for a while . . ."

He paused for effect, and to look at us. He's enough of a businessman to know he'd said some exciting things . . .

"We'd create you into a matador-type thing. Tom Jones with a guitar . . . and the whole slot. We've got the money to do it. We've got the people. We're ready to go. Within a week you'd be on the Johnny Carson show. Within two weeks you'd be in the studios cutting new albums . . . plus T.V. specials, films, the works."

We were flabbergasted.

He flicked the ash from his cigarette. "Well, what do you think?"

Sally and I looked at each other. And in almost the same breath—in unison—we said, "We've got to pray about it . . ."

He about dropped his cigarette.

"What? *Pray* about it! What've you got to pray about?"

I said, "Sid, I've learned that I don't make a move without asking God to direct me . . ."

He shook his head like he thought we were nuts. And in a way we were. Humanly speaking we'd blown it. But by that time God's will had become so important to us that we didn't care.

"Well, okay. Whatever you want to do. You go ahead and draw up your own contract. We want 30% off the top. You take it from there . . ."

The kind of thing he was proposing was unheard of! (Draw up your own contract!) It's the kind of setup that would have made us rich in just a few months. We knew it, and he knew that we knew it. At this point in our Christian lives (looking back now) we can see that Satan was making a last, tremendous attempt to drag us back . . .

But we told him we'd pray about it. Then we went home. And that's exactly what we did. We prayed about it. We really sought the Lord about it. And if you'd been faced with such a decision as this one yourself . . . you'd have done the same thing.

Because we were facing a decision that involved every single facet of our lives . . .

Our professional life.

Our home life.

Our life with Jesus.

Our ministry to the youth.

Razzle dazzle would replace the stability Sally and I held so very dear . . .

You see, we felt, and now I know this is true: we were being tempted of Satan . . .

He was saying, "All this . . . vast areas of public adulation . . . money . . . possessions . . . will I give you . . . if you'll just fall down and worship me . . ."

We felt that he was daring us to cast ourselves from the pinnacle of the temple to ". . . prove God, to see if He'll come and rescue you . . ."

So what did we say when we called Sid back?

We never did call him.

He called us a few days after the meeting. "Well, Chico . . . what's the word?"

"Sid . . . we're still praying. And we still don't know."

"Okay. But keep in touch . . ."

A few more days would pass. "Chico . . . Sally. You know better than anybody else . . . this is a fantastic offer we're making you . . ."

"Yeah, we know that, Sid. But you see . . ."

And I'd tell him that we were trusting God to lead us. It was a totally foreign language to him. He could not comprehend what we were saying when we said, ". . . praying . . . trusting God . . . letting Him lead us . . ."

Frankly, it was the biggest bundle we ever placed on the altar of sacrifice.

But, as it turned out, we never had to make a decision. Sid simply stopped calling.

I know now—even more than I knew then—that had I signed with Sid, it would have been the end. I mean Sid would have owned me, body and soul. He would have told me what to say. Where to go. Who to be seen with. Other women. Other men. We wouldn't have had any choice anymore.

And God would have taken a back seat.

We thank God that the Holy Spirit gave us the guts to turn the whole package over to Him.

We've never been sorry. Never.

Now for the flip side . . .

We had turned down the biggest deal we'd ever seen. We were giving God our total energies at Trinity. The youth group continued to grow.

300 . . . 350 . . . even 500 on occasion. But we were still living on a small salary.

I don't want to embarrass the church. Because I honestly think they thought we had resources to live on. And that the money they gave us was just a token. But what they didn't know was this: we had no income . . . except what they gave us.

So God began pruning some of the chaff away . . . I began taking stuff to the hock shop.

Like radios . . .

And fur coats . . .

And TV's . . .

And jewelry . . .

And cameras . . .

All sorts of stuff. That's just what it was—stuff. Stuff that had been so important to us before. And now God just simply took the desire (and need) for all of it away from us.

I don't think the church knew this. I hope not.

I remember the first time I took my first load of precious junk to that pawn shop.

Sally was embarrassed. "What'll people think?"

"I don't know, Honey. But we gotta eat . . . at least if we're going to keep on serving God . . ."

"Well, I guess you're right."

Some of the stuff we got back. Most of it is still there. I wasn't too concerned about being seen coming out of the pawn shop. Because a lot of people find real bargains there.

But I desperately hoped nobody'd see me taking stuff in. As far as I know they didn't . . .

But during all those months, God supplied our needs. People would hand money to us (which was needed that very day, in that very amount, to pay some payment). Or we'd find an envelope in the mail box with money in it. No name. No way we could thank anybody. But we certainly thanked God.

One Christmas it looked very slim. We had saved a few dollars to buy the kids something— we figured $10 apiece was the limit. It was, too. All we had was $50. Nothing for the tree. Nothing for Christmas dinner.

Then our boy got sick.

We took him to the hospital. And when we left we were $20 short.

"What'll we do?" I asked Sally.

"I don't know, Chico." She smiled her angelic smile. "But I just know God will provide."

He did.

Somebody gave us a permit to cut a tree from the hills. We cut it down. Incidentally it was so big we had to chop and chop and chop when we got home, to get it to fit into our living room. God gave abundantly . . . a bigger tree than we could even use.

In our poverty, God did provide. People began bringing in food. And toys for the children. Gifts for us. Praise God, we ended up with enough food for weeks. The very best Christmas we'd ever had in our entire lives (up to that point). And still God continued to bless our lives.

But in the midst of all this blessing . . . there came a sort of "holy frustration" . . . I guess that's what you'd call it. I was giving God everything I had. So was Sally. But I seemed to be . . . well I was—I was getting out ahead of the Lord.

There had to come a showdown.

17

What's Goin' on, God?

It wasn't long in coming. The showdown.

It had nothing to do with the church. Or the pastor. Or with anybody for that matter. It was just me . . . just between me and God . . .

We had a television show at the church that was going great. I was really digging that. We were syndicating it, and I was helping with that. I was involved with that show, putting together an album . . . we were getting ready to produce a film . . .

Suddenly things began piling up.

I saw that I'd become sort of a Christian PR man. Just busy, busy, busy. Going in circles all the time. I was getting out of sync with the Lord. Getting ahead of Him. Not taking time to listen to Him. Things came to a head on a Friday.

I was supposed to fly out to Reno to do a show at the State Prison in Carson City, Nevada. So I rushed home from the church (on my usual merry-go-round of activities) to get ready to go. Sally was upset with me (with good reason), but I was being very human, very Chico. And God was not in control of me right then . . .

Sally looked at me as I rushed into the house. "Honey," she said, "are you *really* going to go to Reno?"

I said, "Yeah."

She said very softly, "Have you prayed about it?"

"Of course I did!"

The fact that I hadn't really prayed about it . . . and that I'd actually lied to Sally . . . bugged me even more.

I said to myself, *Now what did I do that for? She's right!*

And because she was right and I'd lied to her . . . and was too proud, and too upset to admit it . . . it made me mad. And the more I thought about it the madder I got and the madder I got the more I thought about it.

Finally I jumped on my motorcycle to go for a ride and cool off. I'm not a dirt bike rider by any means. I have a hard time keeping it straight on the street. But I headed out across the desert and kept going faster and faster . . .

Agonizing . . .

Trying to pray . . .

Hating myself . . .

Wishing I was anybody but Chico Holiday . . .

I was really bugged at myself . . .

And everybody else . . .

I finally wound up out at the dump. It's not supposed to be a dump. But a lot of people come out and dump their trash there. I pulled up here. All sorts of trash and garbage lying around. And I parked the bike . . .

I was really miserable.

I picked up a stick and waved it around. I was beside myself.

"What's goin' on, God?" I yelled at the top of my voice.

"What's happening? You told me Your burden was light . . . but I've never had so many hassles in my life . . . till I became a Christian! Something's wrong . . .!"

I walked around, waving that stick. Like Moses on the backside of the desert, I guess.

"I'm doing everything You said I was supposed to do. And look at where I am! I'm messed up . . ."

Never before in my life had I been like this. I'd never talked to God like this. I was desperate. I let it all come out. I don't know how long I argued with God. Or, rather, told God where I was at. Where we were at . . .

"My brains are all scrambled, God! And my family. I don't get to see them. I'm spending all my time at the church . . . peace, joy, happiness, God. I don't know what all that is. I'm nothin' but a big aggravation . . ."

I told him about people calling me with their problems. "But, God, I've got my own problems . . ."

I knew I was yelling. At the top of my lungs. I was serious. It was no act.

"I had it made, God, when I was at the Strip. I had no pressures (a lie, of course). No problems (a bigger lie). I had good money. All I had to do was go to work. Do my job. That was it. I was driving a Lincoln. Now it's a Toyota . . ."

Part of the time I was crying. Then I'd shout.

And all the time I was walking around with that stick in my hand. Waving it. At nothing. Then at God.

"I don't need what I've got, God! I don't need it. You told me I'd have humility . . . you're right. I've never been so humiliated in my life. People give those wonderful, tremendous testimonies—about being zapped with lightning, and hearing the Hallelujah Chorus—and I don't hear anything but complaints . . . and griefs . . . and problems . . .

"People sing the blues to me all day . . . Oh, God, I need help! I've got to have help! Look down on me, God. And help me . . ."

I climbed back on my bike.

I thought a minute. Then I gave God an ultimatum . . .

"I'm out here in the desert for You to give me an experience. *And either You give me an experience I'll never forget . . . or . . . or You and Me are quits.* Either you get it on, or I'm gettin' off . . .! Understand!"

When I quit talking, nothing happened. Nothing. A jack rabbit thumped through the sagebrush. The wind blew a spurt of hot dust across the trail. But God didn't speak to me . . .

I said, "Did you hear me, God? Well, I meant it . . ."

I started my bike and I laid down on the gas. I was hitting 30 or 40 miles an hour. Then I did a stupid thing. If somebody would put a gun to my head, I couldn't tell you why I did it. But all of a sudden I made a sharp turn and headed out through the brush . . .

The desert was strewn with thousands of rocks the size of coconuts. And I headed right for them. I didn't dodge them. I don't know why. I headed right for them . . . throttle wide open . . .

Well, you know what happened.

I must have done a two-and-a-half bank shot with my head off some of those boulders. I really don't know what happened. When I became aware of things again I realized I was in a mess. My head was bleeding. And I was all smashed up . . .

But I still hadn't learned a thing. I still hadn't seen what God was doing.

Somehow I got the bike started. Somehow I got back on it. And somehow I managed to slowly, very slowly, bleeding profusely all the way, ride the bike back to Vegas . . .

Now I really had something to feel sorry for myself about. "See, God, what You made me do . . ." I said. "You made me crack up. You made me miss the plane to Reno . . ."

Sally knew me pretty well. She knew something was terribly wrong. And she'd been out looking for me . . . I got home before she did. I stumbled into the bathroom . . .

The kids saw me. "Daddy, Daddy! You're hurt! Oh, Daddy . . .!"

They knew I was hurt. But at that time I didn't know how badly I was smashed up. I was washing my face off, or trying to, when Sally came in. The kids were crying. And I was beginning to hurt real bad. I was putting some bandages on.

Sally took one look at me. "We're going to the hospital!"

142

"No we're not. I'll be all right!"

"We're going to the hospital," she said. And when Sally speaks like that we . . . well, we went to the hospital.

So, a few minutes later we ended up at the emergency hospital. We had to wait. And while we waited, a bunch of people who had been hurt and burned in a forest fire were brought in. I felt really bad about being there . . . they had been hurt through no fault of their own. But what had happened to me was my own fault.

I said, "Sally, let's not take up time here. There's another hospital around the corner. A private hospital. Let's go there."

You see, that bump on my head was beginning to jar things back into place. Now I was beginning to see things in the right perspective. Just beginning . . .

Sally said, "Not there, Chico. Let's go to the Valley Hospital . . ."

"Sally, we can't go there. We don't have any money. Or insurance. Let's just forget it. Sal, I don't feel so good . . . I can't wait any longer. Let's just go home and I'll go to bed. . ."

She could see that I was really hurt. "No. No," she said. "We're not going home. We're going over to Valley. Don't worry about it. We'll take care of it somehow . . ."

"How? How can we take care of it?" (You see, the Lord hadn't yet shown me that He was the one. He was the provider. Not Chico Holiday.)

"We can take some more things to the pawn shop . . ."

So we went over there.

Let me tell you about that hospital. It's beautiful. It's like walking into a beautiful hotel. Beautiful carpeting. Color coordinated throughout the whole place. Paintings on the wall. I was so sick right then that I didn't think about the cost. But Sally did. And she was praying. Committing it to Jesus.

So they started sewing me up . . . and all at once I began crying . . .

Sally leaned over, very concerned. "Chico, Honey . . . it's going to be all right . . ."

Then I began laughing. Sally looked at me strangely. And I know she must have thought I had flipped. She didn't say anything. She just looked.

"Sally . . . Sally . . . do you want to hear something? *The Lord answered me . . .*"

"What are you talking about?"

"Well, out in the desert . . . well . . . I was mad at God. And I told Him I wanted an experience I would never forget . . . that I wasn't leaving that desert till I got it . . ."

She looked puzzled. I think she thought I was still upset by the shock of it all.

". . . and Sally . . ." I think I began laughing again. "Sally . . . every time I shave I'll remember. I may forget the pain of all this . . ."

I took her finger and ran it over the freshly sewn-up place under my chin.

"But, Sally, I'll never forget this experience. Because God left His signature there on my face. Praise God, Sally! Do you hear what I'm saying? *God left His signature on my face!*

"He did what I asked. He gave me an experience

144

I'll never forget. He loves me so much, Sally . . . so much . . ." For a moment I was overcome with tears and the wonder of it all. "He loves me so much . . . that He wouldn't let me get away from Him . . ."

Sally was crying too. There in the hospital room God did something great for both of us. His Holy Spirit hovered over us . . .

About that time the nurse came in. "Mr. Holiday, you've got some internal injuries, the doctor said. So we'll have to keep you here for a while. At least for the night . . ."

Sally and I looked at each other. Every second the clock ticked sounded like a cash register ringing. We knew this was a very expensive, very exclusive hospital. And we were literally broke. She touched my arm. "Honey, I'm going to call the church. And get people praying . . ."

I didn't know till later how seriously injured I was. But I guess I almost pushed God too far, because I was pretty banged up. I learned all that later. Right now I just let the doctors and nurses take care of me. And I was glad for them.

I really had a rough night. *Apparently God didn't want me to forget that He was still in charge* . . .

The next day a good friend of ours, Phyllis Donovan came in to visit. She and her husband, Bob, were quite new at Trinity, and they were precious friends. She's a lovely lady. But she was rather upset when she saw me.

"I went to the church for something . . . and learned you were in here. What are you doing here?"

She hardly gave Sally or me a chance to answer. She turned to the nurse. "Let me see that chart."

Sally and I thought Phyllis had flipped. What was she doing?

The nurse handed it over with a polite, "Yes, Ma'am."

Phyllis flipped through the chart as though she knew what she was doing. She spoke to the nurse. "Who's the doctor on this case?"

The nurse told her with no hesitation.

"Get him on the phone. I want to talk to him . . ."

The nurse started to leave.

"Just a minute. Before you call him . . . move Mister Holiday to that private intensive care room down the hall . . ."

"Yes, Ma'am." She left quickly

I recovered enough to say, "Look . . . Phyllis. Hold it. This is too expensive as it is . . . we appreciate it. But, this is more than we can handle. I mean, we don't have any money . . . no insurance . . ."

She put her arm around Sally, and touched my arm. "Don't worry about it." She smiled.

"No, Phyllis." I was hurting again, but I had to get this across to her. "Thanks . . . but we just can't . . ."

Sally agreed with me.

Phyllis turned to Sally. "Sally, go downstairs and look at the plaque in the foyer . . ." Sally hesitated. Phyllis smiled. "Go on. Go read it . . ."

Five minutes later Sally was back. Wonder and amazement written on her face. "You . . . I mean, you and Bob . . .?"

Phyllis smiled. By now they were already moving me out of the room. Carefully and expertly. She nodded. "Yes, Bob and I own this place . . . so, you see, it's all right . . ."

They wouldn't take a dime from us for all of that.

Looking back now, I can see the way God handled one of his stubborn kids. I . . . imagine, me, Chico Holiday . . . I was challenging the God of this universe. And He very patiently saying 'Okay, have it your own way.' And He took His hand of protection off me for just a moment. *Just a moment*. And I nearly killed myself. I nearly did. My spleen was ruptured and bleeding. I could have died . . .

But the next day when the doctors checked me over, the bleeding had stopped. Healed! I'm glad God resumed control of my life. You know, He does a much better job than I do.

So I went to Explo '72 in bandages. With a black eye, with my arms and legs all skinned up. Sally covered the worst places on my face with makeup. Most of the results of that crash are all gone now . . .

Except for one . . .

There's still that scar beneath my chin . . .

The one I feel every day when I shave . . .

I'll never forget it . . .

Because that's the place where God left His signature upon my body . . .

So I'll never, never doubt God again.

18

And Now What?

God continually amazes me.

He really does.

He's a whole lot smarter than most folks give Him credit for. Including Chico Holiday.

You see, He can take a stubborn, skinny, Italian (along with all the adjectives you want to use for whatever I am) . . . and He can make something useful out of it. *Out of me!* How did He do it? How can He do it?

I don't know.

I really don't.

I just accept it. And Him. And Jesus. And His wonderful Holy Spirit . . . and all They do. In me. For me. Through me. I mean, it's tremendous how the Holy Spirit takes whatever you give Him—if you really give Him all of yourself—and shapes it into something better than it was . . .

Well, I'm no theologian, so I'll just leave this theological discussion (if, indeed, that's what it is) and get on with the job. You see, I've been learning a lot. I may not have learned much. But I know this:

God isn't finished with me yet. I'm still under construction.

But I'm learning. Praise the Lord, I'm learning . . .

Let me share this with you before I go on: if you really mean business with the Lord . . . well, your life will be a continuous round of excitement and glory.

Excitement because He's new every day. And yet the same.

Glory because He's always letting His Holy Spirit bring new, fresh insights to you through His Word (like Jesus promised in John 14, 15 and 16). He's always bringing new opportunities to you that allow you to share Jesus with somebody . . .

And that's the most exciting thing of all. To share Jesus. To allow the Holy Spirit to just flow through you. To sing in the Spirit. To pray in the Spirit. To give God your heart. Your life. Your home. Your talents (or lack of them, whatever). Your tongue and lips. To just yield yourselves completely to Him.

Something that's so vitalized my life that I can't get over the wonder of it is something that the Apostle Paul speaks of in one of his letters to the Church.

He said, "Be not drunk with wine, wherein is excess; but be filled with the Spirit" (Ephesians 5:18).

That concept. That filling has changed my life. And Sally's. The Holy Spirit did for us what we could not do. He sought us out . . . in show business (and all that entails) . . . in Harold's Club. He gave us a New Song. A New Life. He allowed us to minister that New life . . . to the uttermost parts of the world.

And for that . . . and everything He does, we thank Him. We thank Him with our lives . . . and for the rest of our lives (and that's just the beginning) . . .

Praise the Lord! *Praise the Lord!*

So much has happened since Jesus found us (and we let Him take over our lives) . . . and the Holy Spirit filled us . . . that much of it is a blur . . . a precious, holy blur . . . but I'd like to share some of those flashbacks.

Little miracles. Like when I was attending law school in Las Vegas . . . and my boss at the Thunderbird said, "Chico, you've been working pretty hard. I've noticed you studying between shows . . . your books spread out on the "21" tables . . ."

That was really funny. Customers looking at this crazy kid in a gambling casino, books spread out, studying. *Studying!* But I got my best licks in between midnight and 2:00 a.m.

Sometimes the customers would say, "Working on a new system to beat the game . . .?" I'd just grin and say, "Yeah . . . yeah."

Anyway, Jess said, "Chico, during the finals . . . why don't you take some time off till the exams are over . . ." That was great. A miracle. A little one. But a miracle no less.

Something else. While I was at law school, I saw these real tough-looking dudes one day. Bikers. Looked like Hell's Angels. You know, head bands made of beer can tabs. Levi jackets with the sleeves torn off. Long hair. Tattoos. The whole bit. One of these guys was sketching something on a drawing pad. I thought, *Probably a nude girl on a motorcycle* . . . Out of curiosity, I edged around to take a peep.

Another miracle. This tough biker was sketching a beautiful drawing—tremendously skillfully done, like a steel engraving—of Christ on the Cross. I looked at those "punks" with new respect after that . . .

Sally has always amazed me. *I love that girl so much.* It was she who prayed me out of those upholstered sewers . . . she was the one who brought me to Jesus . . .

She's brought a lot of others to Him, too.

Like that girl in a restaurant one time. Well, let me have Sally tell you the story.

When I saw her that night, God spoke to me. He told me to go and talk to her. You know, you don't just go and tell somebody that God has told you they're planning to commit suicide. But God had told me that.

So I went over and just stood by her chair. Just stood there . . .

Pretty soon she looked up. "Are you people talking about Billy Graham . . . or something . . .?" she asked.

So I sat down. She wanted me to. And she began pouring out her life to me. It was a pretty sordid story. After about an hour of just pouring out to me, she looked up . . . kind of startled . . . questioning, sort of pleading . . . like she really needed somebody.

"But . . ." she sighed and swirled the glass between her fingers. "But . . . you wouldn't understand. You're so pretty . . . and . . . well . . . I guess nobody understands . . ."

I looked at her. "I was a Playboy bunny . . ." That's as far as I got.

"You do understand! You do . . .!"

She was silent for a while. Then I began telling her about Jesus. How He'd changed my life. How He'd set me free . . . and she seemed very distracted. Sometimes I felt she was listening. Other times I didn't. She kept looking at her watch . . .

Finally she said, "I haven't always been this way . . ."

I nodded. "I know."

"This morning when I got up . . . I said, 'God, if You're there You'd better show Yourself . . . because if I don't find something good in my life today . . . before midnight tonight . . . I'm going to destroy myself.'"

She looked at her watch. I looked at mine. *It was exactly midnight!* We talked for another hour, then she said she was okay and that she was going to her room.

The next morning she called me. "Sally . . . maybe you don't think I listened to you last night. But I did. I heard every single word . . . and I do believe that Jesus is the answer. I'm going back to Connecticut to my family . . . I'm going to start a new life. Thanks, Sally. Thanks a lot . . ."

*   *   *

I remember when I was just starting out as a singer, not really knowing who or what Chico Holiday was. I did know that there were three places that were considered "plums." If you could play these places—and do good—you were in . . . Las Vegas, New York and . . . *Melodyland*.

I kept hearing the name—*Melodyland*. It had a nice sound. I learned that it was a very posh theater-in-the-round in Anaheim, California. It was near Disneyland. And that's where the action was . . . it was that kind of a place . . .

I can remember watching the "Johnny Carson Show" and Johnny would ask one of his guests—like Buddy Hackett or Sammy Davis, Jr., "Where will you be next?" The answer would be, "Well, Johnny, next week we'll be in Vegas . . . and then we'll open at *Melodyland*."

And everybody, including me, would say, 'Wow . . .!"

And I would pray (that was before I knew Jesus) . . . "God, let me have just one shot at Melodyland. Let me one day sing at Melodyland . . ."

But in my wildest imaginings I didn't expect God to answer "that prayer." I mean . . . after all . . .

Meanwhile, while I was getting to know Jesus, learning how to minister for Him—things changed at Melodyland. The property owner went broke. And God led a daring, Spirit-led preacher to buy Melodyland! I mean *buy* it. He didn't have any money (I learned all of this later, but it's a tremendous miracle of faith). But this guy, Ralph Wilkerson got a bunch of people steamed up, got them believing God was helping them (and He was, He really was) . . . and they turned it into *Melodyland Christian Center!*

And now that place is about the neatest, goingest place for Jesus there is. You'll be hearing more and more about Melodyland Christian Center . . .

Then came that phone call.

"Chico . . . Chico Holiday . . ."

"Yes. This is Chico . . ."

"This is Ralph Wilkerson . . . Pastor Wilkerson, from Melodyland . . . *Melodyland Christan Center,* in Anaheim . . ."

I wondered if he could hear my quick intake of breath . . .

And I managed to stammer out my usual super-cool reply, "Y . . . y . . . es . . . y-yes . . ."

". . . well, Dick Mills suggested we invite you down for a service. Can you work it into your schedule . . .?"

Could I?

I did some quick arithmetic, scanning my calendar . . .

"Sure. I mean, yes Pastor Wilkerson . . ." and I suggested a couple of dates.

Wilkerson named one, thanked me, and hung up after assuring me of his prayers . . .

I hung up the phone and weakly thanked God.

I could hardly wait to get there . . .

It was tremendous. I mean ministering at Melodyland Christian Center. Pastor Wilkerson . . . the people . . . the ways God is moving . . . tremendous! It was clearly "so right" . . . so clearly God's place for Sally and me that we stayed on. And all I could say when we knew God wanted us to stay (and all I can say about it now), was, "Praise God! Praise the Lord!"

Because *He does answer our prayers.* He really

does! (He'll give you the desires of your heart, providing Jesus is number one. Providing *He* is your motivating force.) Yes . . . He answered my prayer . . . but in a way I'd never dreamed.

But I'm getting ahead of my story. While I was still in Vegas, one day I got a quickly scrawled note from our good friend Dick Mills. (I first met Dick in Reno at a mens' breakfast. Later that night he came to see me in the Lounge at Harold's Club . . . to see—I think, if I was really singing the Jesus songs people were telling him about or what. We became good friends.) And now I'll go on with the story about the note . . .

It read something like this: "Chico, there's this Christian night club up here in Seattle. I've told them all about you and I really feel the Lord would like you to think about it. Dick."

I said to myself, "Christian night club? . . . In Seattle? I've got the best clubs in the world here in Las Vegas! Dick has really gone off the deep end this time." But God was in his suggestion . . . and . . .

Two weeks later I opened at the Sternwheeler, a Christian night club in Seattle. (Praise the Lord for the obedience of Dick Mills.) At the same time I enrolled at the Seattle Bible Training School—and thereby hangs a tale . . .

We had sold our home and bought a little Toyota station wagon. We had planned for a young man to help Sally drive up. But at the last moment he couldn't go. So Sally packed all our worldly goods into the biggest U-Haul she could rent, with a huge trailer behind it. The whole church helped pack the trailer and truck . . .

But just before Sally and the family left, the Donovans came over. Bob looked at the Toyota in horror. "Sally, are you going to drive *that* to Seattle . . .?

Sally said, "Why, yes. Of course."

He said, "Give me the keys." So she did.

A little while later he brought it back—with new tires all around. And, a new reverse. She hadn't told him that the reverse didn't work. But he found out and had it replaced. Praise the Lord for Christian friends like Bob and Phyllis.

So on moving day, Sally loaded all the kids (all five of them) our two dogs and two cats, into the cab of the truck and the Toyota (fairly evenly distributed), gave the Toyota keys to a teenage girl, Terrie, committed the whole thing to God. And took off.

Incidentally, Sally had never driven a truck in her life. She had absolutely no idea about downshifting. She had never even tried to back a trailer, to say nothing of a huge semi-trailer. "But I knew I wouldn't have to back it," Sally told me—after I'd somewhat recovered from the shock of all this. "I just knew that God would let us go 'straight ahead'." And He did.

Before going down a long stretch of very steep grade between Las Vegas and Seattle, God intervened again. The brakes would never have held the truck on that grade. She had driven into a gas station so close to a post that she couldn't drive it out. So she asked a man to back it up for her.

He did. Then he got out and let her climb in

(Sally didn't know at that time that he was a state patrolman in plain clothes). He looked up at her. "Lady," he said, "where are you going?"

"To Seattle."

"Do you know how to drive in the mountains?"

"Oh, yes," she told him.

"Do you know how to downshift?"

"No . . ."

He laced her up one side and down the other for about fifteen minutes. He yelled at her till she really listened. He told her how to downshift. Then he told her to get going. "And don't turn around and come back into Nevada or I'll arrest you! Hear that? Understand?"

"Yes, Sir," very meekly.

So she left. And God taught her how to downshift in the mountains—through that state patrolman. We both praise God for that man. I hope to meet him some day and thank him.

The story of that trip to Seattle would make a book itself. And how God gave us a tremendous home there. Miracle after miracle after miracle. But just one more incident I need to share. To tell you what kind of a woman God gave me for a wife.

Sally had stopped at a station for gas somewhere along the way. An attendant came up, scratching his head when he saw her.

"Lady," he said, "did you pull that rig in here?"

"Yes I did."

He yelled at another man. "Charlie, come here. Look at this. This woman drove this rig in here . . . all by herself. That's the kind of women we need in this world. Women who can do anything."

Sally said he was an old man, maybe in his late 70's or maybe 80. By this time quite a crowd had gathered around the truck-trailer and Toyota.

"I didn't think they made women like her anymore," he told the crowd. Sally was embarrassed, but he kept on . . .

To her he asked, "Are all those your children?"

"Yes . . ."

"Lady, you're terrific! And when you get to Seattle, be sure and tell your husband I told you so!"

I agree.

Sally is terrific. She brought me to Jesus. She led me into the deep things of Jesus and the Holy Spirit. She led me into God's Word. She prayed for me when there was no possibility of me ever leaving the show business rat race I was tied into.

I praise God for the wife he has given me. And I want to dedicate this book to her. Amen!

Well . . . now what?

The rest is history. God gave me the desires of my heart. He miraculously moved us to Melodyland (remember how I'd prayed that He would? And He did . . . in His time, not mine. That trip from Seattle, too, would make a book. Enroute, while I drove, Sally was midwife to our St. Bernard dog, and delivered a nice litter of puppies. Ask us about that sometime.)

We praise God, because He has given us the most exciting challenge there is in the world today . . .

Of singing the glories of Jesus . . .

Of sharing the New Life and the Good News that I have found . . .

Of touching the lives of young people (of all ages) for my precious Lord . . . not just helping people to forget their troubles for an hour or so—like in the old days. Now through the "Good News" I can help them find changed lives—forever. Eternally.

One more thing: this is the last chapter of this book. *But it is not the end.*

Not by any means.

It is only the beginning.

Because Jesus is coming soon. And until He comes . . . every single day is new in Jesus!

"Even so, come quickly, Lord Jesus."

Further information regarding Chico Holiday or Melodyland can be obtained by writing: Melodyland Christian Center, P.O. Box 6000, Anaheim, California 92806.